Good Morning World

Good Morning World

Tim Colliver

BearManorMedia.com

Copyright © 2008 by Tim Colliver
All rights reserved.

Published by:

Bear Manor Media
PO Box 71426
Albany GA 31707

www.bearmanormedia.com
Book Design by Leila Joiner

Printed in the United States of America on acid-free paper

ISBN 978-1-59393-135-3
ISBN 1-59393-135-2

Acknowledgments

Without the help of several people, this book would have never come to print. My sincerest thanks goes out to series creators/producers Bill Persky and Sam Denoff, and to co-star and all-around good guy Ronnie Schell. I deeply appreciated Joby Baker's candor and honesty…and terrific memory for filling in many of the gaps during my research.

There were also other individuals who helped me tremendously in the very early stages of this manuscript. Gary Wedemeyer aimed me in the right direction and without his help I would've never been able to get the interviews I needed. My Canadian friend, Bruce Button, provided me with that great photo of him and Julie Parrish near the end of her life, and I thank him for his help in locating some of the background information on the series. Bob Benedict and his *TV of Your Life* website was unselfish in supplying me with tapes of the series for my research long before the DVD release. If you're a collector of old TV shows, shoot Bob an email.

Lastly, my thanks goes out to the best publisher in the world, Ben Ohmart and Bear Manor Media. Without Ben's belief in this project, all of my research would've been for naught. And the reason this little book looks SOOOO good is because of Leila Joiner's efforts in typesetting and layout.

Now for the legal stuff…

It is not the intention of the author or publisher to infringe upon the copyright or ownership of *Good Morning World*, but only to tell the story of the history, creation, and production of this TV series.

All photographs used in this book are courtesy of CBS/Paramount Productions unless otherwise noted.

Information relating to ratings are courtesy of the A.C. Neilsen Company.

Episode descriptions are taken from program listings that appeared in *TV Guide* magazine. Other material such as photographs, commentary, and information referenced to *TV Guide* came from various issues throughout the 1967-68 season and are courtesy of that publication.

Table of Contents

GOOD MORNING WORLD: 9
   BEHIND THE SCENES OF THE 1967 CBS SITCOM

CHAPTER 1: 12
   IN THE SHADOW OF MT. VAN DYKE ...

CHAPTER 2: 21
   (RE) CASTING CALL

CHAPTER 3: 34
   BEHIND THE SCENES

CHAPTER 4: 47
   GOOD MORNING WORLD EPISODE GUIDE

CHAPTER 5: 94
   "CANCELLATION *REALLY* WASN'T
   THAT BAD A DEAL AFTER ALL…"

CHAPTER 6: 107
   A LOOK BACK ...

Good Morning World:

Behind the Scenes of the 1967 CBS Sitcom

It is mid-February 1968. Among the casualties of the just-completed TV season is *Good Morning World,* the first television show to deal with the workings of a radio station and its two morning disc jockeys. The way that *TV Guide* described it in a June 1968 article, one of only a pair of articles the publication ever did on the show, one of the series' co-stars strides into the commissary of Desilu Studios, head held high and flashing what has come to be known as his "terrier grin."

Photo courtesy TV Guide

"Well, gang, you lose a few and—you lose a few," announces Ronnie Schell in a voice that mimics Don Adams' classic secret agent Maxwell Smart. The thirty-six-year-old actor/comedian grabs a plate and makes his way down the cafeteria line. "The irony of showbiz—we get cancelled and *Lassie* is renewed for the fifteenth year!"

In the true style of a stand-up comic, which is his background, that last line gets him his laugh from those setting at the table, which include names familiar to every TV viewer this season; Andy Griffith, Kaye Ballard, Ted Bessell and *Good Morning World's* own creator/producer/writer team of Bill Persky and Sam Denoff.

Denoff shakes his head at the remark, half in irritation that Schell's assessment is correct and half with the same regard that one would have for a teasing kid brother.

Ted Bessell, currently riding high on the success of the other Persky/Denoff creation, *That Girl,* looks over at his fellow actor. "What happened?" he asks, a tone of sincere disappointment in his voice.

Schell changes character, his eyes narrowing as he contemplates a conspiracy theory. "It happened like this," he begins, gazing in faux thoughtfulness across the room, elbows on the table and fingers interlaced with thumbs under his chin. "Viewers had their choice between our show and *Tuesday Night at the Movies*." He leans back and waves a hand in a broad sweeping motion and continues, "And all over America people would ask themselves the *big* question: who should we watch tonight—Ronnie Schell ... or Cary Grant?"

The small crowd at the makeshift dinner theatre chuckle among themselves and the conversation changes to other subjects, both personal and professional.

Life goes on and disappointment will fade in the face of new career opportunities. Despite outward appearances, though, Schell is somewhat discouraged that his first true starring role in a TV series should end this way. He described himself as "America's fastest slowest-rising comedian." *TV Guide* called him "the lame duck actor with the happy quack."

Whatever the reason for the demise of *Good Morning World*, America will still be able to watch his antics in front of and behind the mike as the series remains in reruns throughout the summer of '68.

Allow me to tell you a story about how a television show changed a little boy's life ... and while I'm at it, the making of that TV show. This little boy, who was all of nine years old at the time, really didn't know what he wanted to be when he grew up. Whenever the grownups around him would ask, he would give the usual answers typical of a boy his age; "I want to be a fireman, or a policeman, or a doctor ... or maybe go to work for the highway department like my Dad."

But after September 5, 1967, thanks to a TV series called *Good Morning World*, something clicked in the mind of this young child. No longer was being a fireman, policeman, doctor or anything else for that matter an option. From this point forward something new began brewing in his mind that for years to come would firmly focus him on what he wanted to be "when he grew up."

A radio DJ.

Even after *Good Morning World* had been cancelled, a seed was planted and took root. Throughout his teen years whenever someone would ask, be it a relative or a high school guidance counselor, what his career goals were, he would always reply without hesitation:

"I want to be a radio DJ."

Now, I know this guy *really* well, so I can speak with a degree of authority. I know his wife and kids, where he's worked, what he's done, the highs and lows of his life ... and what he stands for.

I know all of this because that little boy ... was me.

There were three times growing up that I was allowed to stay up past my usual nine o'clock bedtime. One was whenever the movie *It's a Mad, Mad, Mad, Mad World* was on. My mother absolutely *loved* that movie and we'd set up and cackle like two kids in a theatre until almost midnight when it was on. Another was in December 1972 when Apollo 17 lit up the night sky in Florida. I was a teenager then and informed my parents there was no way I was missing Gene Cernan and his crew as they took America to the moon for the last time. Lastly, I was expected to hit the sack promptly at ten on Tuesday nights after *Good Morning World* was over.

With this book, I hope you'll set back and let me take you through the history of an obscure, largely forgotten ... little gem of a TV show that literally changed my life. It's a fascinating slice of television history that is told not only from the viewpoint of a fan but also from those that were on the show.

Sociologists are quick to blame television for many of society's ills today ... the violence, the sex, the blurring of traditional family values ... and they may have a point. But I also know from watching the rare reruns of *Good Morning World* and in reading the old *TV Guide* listings that if it hadn't been for this CBS sitcom from so long ago, it's hard to tell how my life would've turned out. In fact, I owe Joby Baker, Ronnie Schell, Julie Parrish, Billy De Wolfe ... and let's not forget Bill Persky and Sam Denoff ... a debt that I can never repay.

Photo courtesy CBS/Paramount

Then again, maybe I can.

Maybe ... perhaps ... this book is my way of letting that little boy I knew so long ago say a heartfelt "thank you" to a bunch of people and a TV series that gave him direction as to what he wanted to be ...

"... when he grew up."

Chapter 1:

In the Shadow of Mt. Van Dyke …

In June 1955, a twenty-three-year-old writer named Bill Persky joined the staff at New York City radio powerhouse WNEW in the continuity department. His salary was a then whopping $35 a week. "Continuity" is radio-speak for writing commercials, "spots" as we call them. Persky's duties also included writing public service announcements and anything else that the announcers would be needing in their copy books during their day-to-day shows. This was in the era when almost everything, except for the music, was done live on the air. It would be another seven years before William Lear would perfect the four-track tape cartridge, which the radio industry would embrace as the broadcast cartridge or "cart." With the cart, which resembled the old 8-track tape, the live radio commercial would be replaced by the slick-sounding highly produced spots we hear today. The cart would in turn meet its demise by the mid-1990s, when computers and digital audio production invaded the radio studio.

Job turnover, then as now, was infamous in radio and Persky found himself getting a promotion when someone left his department … and a raise to $38 a week. He was joined a month later by another writer in the form of twenty-seven-year-old Sam Denoff. WNEW wasn't aware that the young writer they had hired had some broadcasting experience … well, sort of.

"Sam's previous job was as the bargain broadcaster at Cline's Department Store," Persky remembered, "and he could be heard saying, 'attention shoppers, a carload of Maidenform bras at half price has just been delivered to aisle seven on the third floor.'" Denoff was already carving out a niche in department store lore long before 'attention K-mart shoppers' became a household phrase.

Persky found a kindred spirit in Denoff and soon the pair was the best of friends. That friendship found its way into the commercials and announcements they were writing and soon they were bouncing ideas off one another, both for the commercial material that went on the air and some of the comedy material they came up with just for fun.

During the pair's days at WNEW, they got to be great friends with the legendary "Willie-B," William B. Williams, who did a midday and early evening show on the New York City AM station. Williams was a superstar even by today's standards and is credited with carrying on the pioneering radio show *Make Believe Ballroom*, by all measures the first disc jockey show.

Unlike today, radio's biggest product in the fifties and sixties was the guy on the air broadcasting live. Both the audience and the artists who sang on the records bowed down at the altar of the radio DJ and Williams was one of the industry's high priests.

Like most of us in the business, Williams did work outside the station …"voice-overs" as they're called. His voice was heard mostly on TV commercials, but he also did the occasional movie trailer. This led to him being the announcer on Sammy Davis, Jr's. short-lived variety and talk show that was in syndication in the late sixties.

It was Williams who gave Frank Sinatra the moniker "the chairman of the board." When Sinatra had a new single, he'd bring a copy to the station, personally sit down with Williams and talk about it on the air. They became great friends, so much so that when Sinatra's career was in a downturn before his role in the hit movie, *From Here to Eternity*, Williams would have him on his show as often as possible to keep him in the public eye.

Photo courtesy WNEW archives

"He was the one solely responsible for keeping the Sinatra name alive while Frank's career was in a low point before he won an Academy Award for *From Here to Eternity*," Denoff said. "Willie really kept him going by having him on the show with him as often as he could." What people didn't know was how much that debt of gratitude would be wholeheartedly returned in later years when Williams' health began declining.

"Willie had some sort of blood disease," Denoff recalled, "and Frank would send a plane for him and jet him to anywhere in the country so he could get the best medical care available … nobody ever knew about that, but that's how much Frank loved the guy."

The only time Denoff recalled there ever being any tension between the two was when Sinatra found out Williams was dating Frank's ex-wife, actress

Ava Gardner, but in the end it was passed off with a good laugh between the two and only served to forge a stronger friendship.

William B. Williams passed away on August 3, 1986.

Radio has always been on the cutting edge of programming innovations and the management that was in place at WNEW didn't shy away from new ideas. Persky and Denoff found a friend in General Manager John Van Buren Sullivan, affectionately known by the pair as "Silver Jack."

"We were lucky all along the way, Billy and I, with the people we worked for," Denoff related. "Jack Sullivan was our boss for most of the time we were there." Sullivan got the nickname from his silver white hair and sideburns. A tall, handsome man in his mid-fifties, Sullivan was always open to Persky and Denoff's ideas for commercials and public service announcements ... and later comedy efforts at the station as well. His attitude was 'give it a try' and if it worked, great ... if it didn't, so what, tomorrow is another day.

During the station's Christmas party in 1955, the duo came up with a comedy routine that poked fun at both the air staff and management. At that Christmas party, in addition to family and friends, was another onlooker that not only enjoyed the routine but was very impressed with Persky and Denoff themselves.

"It happened there was a young agent there from the Morris Agency," Persky said. "He had just gotten a promotion from the mail room and signed us as his first clients." Their young agent turned out to be none other than George Shapiro, better-known today as the manager for comedian Jerry Seinfeld.

"That's how this whole career of ours started," Denoff added. "We worked with these people who would put their arms around us, guys like Jack Sullivan and later Carl Reiner and Sheldon Leonard ... they were terrific."

WNEW became not only the springboard for the future success of Persky and Denoff, but also became the birthing place for their TV creation some twelve years later. The comedy skit the pair had written for that 1955 Christmas party became the pattern for what would evolve into *Good Morning World*. The two morning DJ's that formed the basis for the series' storylines was loosely based on the morning antics of one of New York's top-rated morning shows.

"Gene Klaven and Dee Finch did the morning show," Persky said. "They were probably the two best morning guys in radio, for my money at least ... and what they did on the air was what we based *Good Morning World* on."

Finally, check out one of the closing credits on any *Good Morning World* episode. It reads "The title *Good Morning World* originated by William B.

Williams." Williams used to open his midday show with "Good Morning World, this is Willie B on WNEW." When Persky and Denoff were searching for a title for their new TV series, they asked their old friend for permission to use his radio sign-on.

By 1960, Persky and Denoff packed it up and went to Los Angeles when they were hired as writers for *The Steve Allen Show* for the princely sum of $500 per week ... but only with the guarantee of a three-week contract.

"I mean it was a crazy thing to do," Persky said. "But as it turned out it was gonna be the best job we had."

It was a performance-based contract. If Steve Allen's people liked the writers' work, they would get picked up for another three weeks. At that point, the pair's contract would be renewed for an additional seven weeks to round out the first half of the TV season. The big *IF* was would they get renewed for the final thirteen weeks to complete the season? Persky and Denoff knew they *had* to be good or it was back to New York with their tails between their legs.

According to Persky, "As it turned out, we were working on the second show of the season and we wrote a joke that Steve Allen liked so much, he went ahead and signed us for the entire season right then and there." The only problem was *The Steve Allen Show* was cancelled after just ten episodes. However, the pair of writers had a contract and was paid for the entire twenty-six-week season, which allowed them to hang around the studios and plan their next move.

Like other out-of-work actors and writers waiting on their next "big break," both men worked a variety of in-between jobs throughout 1961 and into 1962 before landing on *The Andy Williams Show*. With that variety show lasting a year, and realizing that writing for situation comedies would be more lucrative, they turned their efforts into writing scripts for sitcoms. That in itself proved to be a challenge since the thinking at the time was that variety shows and sitcoms were two completely different animals and if you were a writer for a variety show, chances are you couldn't write for a situation comedy. But in looking out over the television landscape of the early 1960s, they saw variety shows as few and far between and situation comedies popping up everywhere.

"We had met Tim Conway on the old *Steve Allen Show*," remembered Denoff. "In fact, we wrote the first joke he ever did on network television." Conway was co-starring on *McHale's Navy* and helped get them an assignment to do a script for that series. This in turn led to every comedy writer's dream assignment ... the "Holy Grail" of the early 1960s ... writing for *The Dick Van Dyke Show.*

"We had written a sample script for the *Van Dyke Show,*" Persky related. "George Shapiro got it to Carl Reiner and he liked our style." Although Reiner didn't particularly care for the script, he gave them an assignment to write an episode.

"We did the one where Rob is convinced they brought the wrong baby home from the hospital," Persky said, speaking of the classic episode where Van Dyke's character is positive the hospital gave them the wrong baby and invited the couple, who he thinks has their baby, over to their house. The look on his face and the studio audience's uncontrolled laughter when black actor Greg Morris steps through the door is timeless.

After writing that script, Persky said that Reiner wanted to give them an office so they'd have a place to hang out during the series. "He told us he couldn't pay us anything but we could write as many episodes as we wanted." Persky and Denoff became part of the show and went on to write fourteen episodes that season.

When *The Dick Van Dyke Show* went off the air, a ratings champ in 1965, Bill Persky and Sam Denoff were the proud recipients of a pair of Emmy Awards for their work on the series. In just six short years, the pair had come up the ranks from a pair of cancelled variety series, through unemployment and odd jobs, to recognized masters in the business of writing for situation comedies.

"We were the darlings of the world when that show went off," Persky said. "We could've gotten anything we wanted." What Persky and Denoff got was a phone call from the sponsor of *The Dick Van Dyke Show*, consumer products giant Proctor & Gamble. They wanted another hit TV show. And they got one.

That Girl starred Marlo Thomas as a young single woman and an aspiring actress with the storylines concerning all the things she inadvertently got her and boyfriend Donald (played by Ted Bessel) into. The Persky/Denoff creation debuted in the fall of 1966 and not only enjoyed good ratings but also became practically a cultural icon and role model for teenage girls and young women of the late sixties and early seventies.

With *That Girl* enjoying good ratings and audience reviews, Proctor & Gamble came calling to see if Persky and Denoff could work their magic again. As opposed to television shows today, where an advertiser simply buys commercial spots during a program, at that time major corporations would sponsor entire shows and the network for the most part answered to the needs and requests of that sponsor. In the case of *The Dick Van Dyke Show* and *That Girl,* the primary sponsor was Proctor & Gamble.

How much power and influence did the sponsor wield? Denoff recalled what happened when CBS cancelled *The Dick Van Dyke Show* after only one season.

"Carl and Sheldon went to Cincinnati with a guy from the William Morris agency to meet with the head of Proctor & Gamble's television office." Reiner and Leonard knew deep down that *The Dick Van Dyke Show* was a hit just waiting to happen and went to bat for their fledgling show after CBS had cancelled it.

"They went to Cincinnati and met with a Mr. Halverstad, who was in charge of their TV projects." Denoff described Halverstad as a conservative Midwesterner with wire-rimmed glasses, resembling the classic painting by Grant Wood entitled "American Gothic"; the rural couple stood in front of their farmhouse, neither one smiling and the man held a pitchfork.

Reiner and Leonard pleaded their case with Halverstad, convincing him that *The Dick Van Dyke Show* was indeed a quality show, had the potential for a three-to-five-year run to the benefit of Proctor & Gamble and should never have been cancelled. The P & G exec agreed and placed a call to Jim Aubrey, who at the time was responsible for who got renewed and cancelled at CBS. Aubrey was "glad" that Halverstad had called and asked what he could do for him. Keep in mind that at that time, the network knew how to play "step and fetch" with any sponsor that paid big money for programming. It was a case of being told to jump and then asking how high.

"The conversation began with 'We want *The Dick Van Dyke Show* back on,'" Denoff said of Halverstad's phone call. Aubrey replied that the decision had already been made to cancel it.

According to Denoff, there was a long silence, followed by Halverstad coolly replying, "Perhaps you didn't hear me the first time … we want the Van Dyke show back on." There was one other "request" from the voice on the other end of the line. "And when it's back on the air," Halverstad continued, "we want it to follow *The Beverly Hillbillies* for the first six months."

Aubrey hemmed and hawed but had to relent to the demands of the sponsor who was paying the bills and his salary. "Aubrey did it, the audience sampled it and before you knew it … BOOM! … the show became a major hit," Denoff added.

Sponsors and their advertising agencies often came by the studio to check up on their investment, "not to interfere with anything, but just to be around the stars," Denoff said. Later on, some of those people went on to become major players in future television productions. Persky and Denoff were friendly with one man from Benton & Bowles that would visit the set of *That Girl*. "Grant Tinker came out to the set sometimes and one day he caught sight of Mary Tyler Moore and said 'ooooooooo'... and the rest is history." He not only had a hand in Moore's ascent to stardom, but married her as well.

In the summer of 1966, Persky and Denoff had a meeting with the television production executives at Proctor & Gamble and shared with them their proposal for another TV series. There was no doubt it would be a situation comedy but this time around, it would have a uniquely different premise, something that had never been featured on television before ... and wouldn't be again until 1978.

It would be a sitcom about a pair of morning radio disc jockeys and their high-jinx adventures inside and outside the radio station they worked at. The two writers pitched their premise to a receptive P & G television department.

"We told them about our days in radio," Persky said, "and they loved the idea." P & G liked it so much that they guaranteed them a full twenty-six-episode run even before seeing what is called the "premise pilot," that is, the first show of a TV series that introduces the characters and situation, in addition to setting the stage for the episodes to follow.

"That sort of thing is unheard of today," Denoff laughed. "To be guaranteed twenty-six episodes right off the bat and they haven't even seen what the show will look like, but that's the kind of clout the sponsor had back then ... and I guess the confidence they had in me and Billy."

"Originally, pilots were the first episode of how everybody met," Persky said in describing the concept of the pilot episode, where the premise of the series is laid out. "What they found was your cast's performance improved immeasurably as they did more shows." The least perfect episode was usually the pilot and due to its sequential nature, the pilot was usually the first show of the series. "The way we got around that was we took our pilot show and turned it into a flashback later in the season." Persky noted that today many series don't have the traditional pilot episode and instead simply start at some distant point without showing how the characters got together.

The casting call went out for the pilot episode of their newly titled *Good Morning World* and when everything was in place, production began in December. Both producers set high standards for their productions and had no room for the egos and eccentricities that seems to riddle the performing arts. Persky had an unwritten rule when it came to actors: "We must never work with anybody who comes with a set of instructions on them."

In the co-starring role as central character David Lewis was a young actor named Ron Rifkin, with Sharon Farrell playing his wife Linda. Sitting in the director's chair was veteran actor/director Jerry Paris from the old *Dick Van Dyke Show*. At the time of shooting the *Good Morning World* pilot, Rifkin's resume was slim at best with an appearance on Sally Field's *Gidget* as one of its highlights. Farrell, on the other hand, had an extensive list of credits on several familiar series dating back to 1962, even a regular role as "Polly" in *Saints and Sinners* from the same year.

"We found this terrific young guy, Ron Rifkin, who was just wonderful," Persky remembered. "But the powers-that-be discovered he was Jewish, and at that time, that was something that just wasn't gonna happen." There was an unspoken prejudice in place at that time in the industry and to have an ethnic or religious minority in a starring role was a rarity. It wasn't right then and isn't right now, but that's just the way things were. True, there were exceptions to the rule, one of them being Richard Benjamin, who would be starring in *He & She*. For Rifkin, his Jewish heritage became strike one.

Strike two came from the person with the vision as to how the show should look, in this case the guy sitting in the director's chair. Jerry Paris had been both a director on *The Dick Van Dyke Show* and played the role of Rob Petrie's neighbor. Now he was directing the premise pilot of *Good Morning World* and it was becoming an intense atmosphere on the set, the last thing you want when doing a situation comedy.

"Jerry could be a very destructive kind of guy," Persky said in describing the pilot's production. "Carl used to say most people have a tape delay from their brain to their mouth of about a second and a half and Jerry didn't." Some of the things that Rifkin and Farrell were hearing from the director's chair weren't helpful and guiding, but were caustic and hurtful. This isn't to say that Paris was a mean and vengeful person, because he wasn't. But when the creativity is flowing and the brain is in overdrive, things are said and done that perhaps wouldn't have been if there was a "tape delay" in place. (It's like what a friend of mine who worked in television once told me. "You radio guys operate at a different level than the rest of us," he said. "Everyone else runs at sixty cycles," referring to normal household electrical current. "You guys in radio run at like ninety!")

Paris was humming along at close to a hundred and when that was coupled with Rifkin's inexperience … he was all of twenty-seven and fairly new to the business … the pilot just didn't come out like it should have. "Jerry wasn't a bad guy," Persky said in Paris' defense. "He was just the wrong guy to be directing Ron, who was scared to death ... I mean here was this young Jewish kid in the lead of a TV series pilot, had just gotten to L.A., and was being directed by this intense guy who had been around the block more than a few times."

Both Persky and Denoff admit that Paris' direction, combined with Rifkin's inexperience, produced a pilot that just wasn't as light and airy as the first show of a situation comedy should be. As much as ethnicity and professional differences came into play, the fact remained that the performances on *Good Morning World's* first pilot weren't as good as they could have been. It wasn't surprising then that when the programming types at CBS watched it, they rejected it.

Under normal circumstances that should have been strike three and you're out. However, since Proctor & Gamble had already committed to twenty-six episodes and CBS really did like the premise, the network made a request that put *Good Morning World* into the ranks of an elite handful of TV shows.

CBS wanted to see a second pilot episode.

Chapter 2:

(Re) Casting Call

After CBS rejected the first *Good Morning World* pilot, Persky and Denoff scratched their heads, made some minor changes to the script, considered changing the title and hired another director. The old adage "a new broom sweeps clean," which they remembered so well from their days in radio, held true as they also hired a new cast. The only holdover from the Rifkin/Farrell pilot was Billy De Wolfe, who reprised his role as stuffy station manager Roland B. Hutton. Both men had the highest regards for the veteran actor/comedian and quickly fell in love with his on- and off-screen quirks. Bill Persky had been a longtime fan of the actor.

"We had written an episode of the *Van Dyke* show called 'The Ugliest Dog in the World,'" Persky remembered of the October 1965 show that featured his friend. "That's where we first met Billy and in this script we wrote, Rob needs this really ugly dog for their show and when they're all done, he realizes no one has made any plans for it after they're finished." In the episode Van Dyke's character decides to take the animal to a "dog beauty parlor," that is run by Rex Spaulding, who is none other than the persnickety "busy-busy-bizzee" Billy De Wolfe.

Denoff added, "He was so prim and proper, but at the same time so damn funny!" De Wolfe was a veteran of the theatre and a true professional but had the unique ability to get his point across if he needed to. "He could cut you up like a stiletto into little pieces and you'd never realize it even when you saw yourself bleeding to death ... he was that piercing with his analysis and his humor ... he was an old pro."

De Wolfe, whose real name was William Andrew Jones, was already sixty years old when production on the second pilot began in January 1967. His career began as a musical

Photo courtesy CBS/Paramount

comedy performer when he was in his teens during the days of Vaudeville. He took the name "Billy De Wolfe" from the manager of the theater in Quincy, Massachusetts where he was born and where he later worked as an usher after school. The son of Welsh immigrants, he broke into show business as a dancer with The Jimmy Cannon Band before touring Europe as both a dancer and satirist. Fame and fortune would come to him in the nightclub circuit and Broadway performances throughout the 1930s and 1940s, where he portrayed eccentric, somewhat effeminate male characters. Hal Erickson's *All Movie Guide* describes his best-known role as that of "Mrs. Murgatroyd," where the mustachioed De Wolfe would be dressed in a wide-brimmed flowery hat and steel-rimmed glasses, impersonating a middle-aged woman doing lunch after a shopping spree. He repeated the role in the 1946 Paramount film *Blue Skies*. De Wolfe made his motion picture debut three years earlier playing the role of "Mr. Bones" in the Bing Crosby film *Dixie* before serving in the Navy.

From there, it was on to other movie roles during the 1940s and 1950s such as *The Perils of Pauline, Duffy's Tavern, Tea for Two* and *Call Me Madam* before breaking into television playing himself on an early Ed Sullivan *Toast of the Town* in 1951. That led to being a regular on *The Imogene Coco Show* in 1954 and transitioning into the growing medium of television all through the rest of the decade. De Wolfe enjoyed stardom on Broadway as well in *Almanac* and *The Ziegfeld Follies of 1957*.

Prior to *Good Morning World*, De Wolfe appeared in the 1965 Patty Duke film *Billie* and in episodes of *Burke's Law* with Gene Barry and *Bob Hope Presents The Chrysler Theatre* that same year. After shooting the revised *Good Morning World* pilot, he appeared in an episode of the short-lived TV series *Rango* in February 1967 and was featured in the highly-rated *That Girl*, another Persky/Denoff creation.

The remaining three co-stars were new faces to the revamped pilot, but not to theatregoers and television viewers. Replacing Ron Rifkin in the leading role of disc jockey David Lewis was a slightly older actor named Joby Baker. Baker

Photo courtesy CBS/Paramount

felt then and now that P & G and CBS should have gone with Rifkin as the series lead.

"They should have got him," Baker said in retrospect. "Ron Rifkin is a terrific actor and would've really brought life to the character of Dave Lewis."

The thirty-three-year-old native of New York was born in Montreal, Canada on March 26, 1934 while his parents were there on business. Three years later tragedy struck the Baker household when his mother passed away and his father, grief stricken, went to Honolulu to spend time with his brother, taking three-year-old Joby with him.

"While he was there, he met a woman who would help him realize life has to go on, and later married my stepmother," Baker remembered of his childhood in the Hawaiian Islands years before statehood. All was well until Sunday morning December 7, 1941. "I was there with my family ... my father and stepmother, when the Japanese bombed us in Honolulu." After the attack and the formal declaration of war the following day, seven-year-old Joby and his mother were evacuated to a new life in California. His father passed away at the age of forty in 1945 when Joby was eleven.

"It was my father's wish, somewhere along the line, that I do this," Baker said. "I can only remember certain things about him but I do remember he wanted me to

Photo courtesy CBS/Paramount

go into performing." He was raised in Los Angeles and attended Fairfax High School. After high school it was on to L.A. City College, and with the encouragement of his mother, Baker embarked on a career in show business.

"I was seventeen or eighteen when I went on the road as a nightclub entertainer doing impressions," he said of those early days, employing props and funny hats in his act. The road shows served as a springboard to better things. "Then I opened at the Sahara Hotel in Las Vegas with Abbott and Costello before going under contract to Columbia Studios and sometimes getting loaned to MGM."

Baker would rack up a long and impressive list of credits in both film and television dating back to 1955 when he appeared in the motion picture *Target Zero* while serving in the Army with his old friend, and later movie superstar, Charles Bronson. Many thought Baker bore an uncanny resemblance to comedian Jerry Lewis and during his career, he could lapse into serious and comedic roles with the ease and skill reminiscent of Dean Martin's old partner.

Throughout the remainder of the 1950s and into the 1960s, his resume was a "who's who" of character appearances on hit television shows of the period. You'll see his name turning up in guest roles several times on both *Dragnet* and *Alfred Hitchcock Presents*. Other shows that featured his talents included *SurfSide 6*, *Bachelor Father*, *Perry Mason* and *Dr. Kildare*. His movie credits were just as impressive.

His role of Myron Malkin in 1959's *The Last Angry Man* made those inside and outside of Hollywood stand up and take notice. Baker said a lot of people auditioned for the character. "Every actor in town wanted that part and Paul Muni saw my test and said, 'I want him.'"

Photo courtesy CBS/Paramount

Baker was at the Latin Casino in Las Vegas at the time, opening for singer Johnny Mathis when he got word that he landed the part. "When I finished up Latin Casino, I hopped a train for Manhattan and started a movie." *The Last Angry Man* became Joby Baker's breakout role.

What followed were three supporting roles in *Gidget*, *Gidget Goes Hawaiian* and *Gidget Goes to Rome*; 1960's *The Wackiest Ship in the Army*, 1965's *When the Boys Meet the Girls* and Elvis' *Girl Happy* and *The Adventures of Bullwhip Griffin* in 1967. It was during filming on *Girl Happy* that Baker met and later married his first wife, actress Joan Blackman.

In the early to mid-1960s, the Western was popular fare and Baker had guest slots on perennial favorites like *Wagon Train* and *Gunsmoke*, and showed up in a March 1967 episode of *Death Valley Days* after finishing the second *Good Morning World* pilot.

Baker described how he got the show. "I was doing a play in Los Angeles, an evening of trilogies by Ray Bradbury." One of his roles was that of an elderly gentleman who was eighty-five years old in *The Man in the Ice Cream Suit*. Another of the characters he played that evening was a Mexican, an uncouth type who lived in a rough neighborhood. "Carl Reiner, Sheldon Leonard, Billy and Sam came down and saw me in this play and thought I was really good ... little did they know I was a better Mexican than I was a regular person."

"The word was out that this play I was in was really a great evening and all these guys showed up, but I didn't know that they were out there," Baker said about that particular evening. "Dick Van Dyke was going off the air and Procter & Gamble wanted them to come up with another Dick Van Dyke guy." Reiner and the gang loved Baker's Mexican character and decided to include the actor in some future *Dick Van Dyke* episodes. "They wrote three Van Dyke shows with me in it to see how I would work out." They were ninety-nine and 44/100th-percent sure Baker was their man, but wanted to be certain he was right for the format.

"The best episode was one called 'Viva Petrie,' where I played the cook for a Mexican bullfighter," Baker said. "And they were all excited about how it went and that's how I got *Good Morning World*."

The popularity of TV shows with a war theme and the situation comedy helped to acquaint viewers with Baker's rising star, in particular his role as "Kelly" on Combat! in the 1962-63 season and those appearances on *The Dick Van Dyke Show* during '65-'66. It was there that Carl Reiner and Sheldon Leonard got their first 'up close and personal' look at the young actor ... and they liked what they saw.

"Joby was an actor/comedian/performer that we had seen in New York and Los Angeles," Persky remembered of the multi-talented artist, who in real life actually was a self-taught artist and painter who worked in oils and pastels. "He had done those *Van Dykes* with us and Carl really loved Joby's work."

The ethnicity question may have prevented Ron Rifkin from getting the part, but it didn't hinder Joby Baker, even though he was Jewish as well. "I got word that there was something with Rifkin regarding the first pilot," Baker said. "Ron was angry afterwards because he must have suspected that that was part of the reason he never got the role." In any event, the Jewish Rifkin was replaced by an equally Kosher Baker, who remembered all those roles when he played a Mexican. "I fooled everybody, including Proctor & Gamble ... they probably thought I really was a Mexican from California or some white guy from Hawaii!"

The other half of *Good Morning World*'s fictional Lewis and Clark Show, that of disc jockey Larry Clark, was played by actor and stand-up comedian Ronnie Schell. He came on the scene for the re-casted second pilot when Reiner's people approached Dick Linke, Schell's manager at the time.

"They told him they liked my work on *Gomer Pyle* and they knew me from the nightclubs," Schell said, who also was recognized from appearances on *The Merv Griffin Show* and *The Tonight Show*. "And they were wondering if I'd be willing to drop *Gomer Pyle* and come on *Good Morning World* ... it was one those classic 'offers you can't refuse.'"

The Richmond, California native son and former semi-pro baseball player, who had just turned thirty-five the previous December 23, was the one most at ease in front of a studio audience and in retrospect, probably should have been *Good Morning World*'s main character. He got his first taste of being in front of an "audience" in high school, notorious for being the class clown and often being sent home from school for his antics. Enlisting in the Air Force brought some discipline to Schell's life but he also was doing stand-up comedy there too, in addition to emcee work and pantomiming records. He volunteered to emcee a variety show to get out of KP duty and found himself touring as a comic with the Air Force's dance band Airmen of Note. Although their paths never crossed, he heard of another guy doing much the same thing in an Air Force uniform ... somebody named Jerry Van Dyke.

Photo courtesy CBS/Paramount

Upon leaving military service, he enrolled at San Francisco State University and while a senior there, started to take his act to a higher level.

"I started working at a nightclub on the north beach of San Francisco called The Purple Onion," Schell remembered. "I auditioned and got the job and with me on the bill was a new comedienne named Phyllis Diller, who was just starting out, and The Kingston Trio." After the Kingston Trio got a recording contract, the nightclub signed an up-and-coming comedy team consisting of two brothers named Tom and Dick Smothers. "That place was the starting point for a lot of new acts in the years to come, people that went on to became really famous ... myself included, of course." He also appeared at another launching pad for comedy acts, the legendary Hungry "i" nightclub.

In the late 1950s, Schell was a featured comedian in Las Vegas. In the early 1960s, he made the move to television and found a willing outlet for a comedian who could also act. After appearances on *The Merv Griffin Show* and several TV commercials, Schell landed a guest character appearance on *The Andy Griffith Show* before scoring a regular supporting role on *Gomer Pyle, U.S.M.C.* as Gomer's bunkmate, Duke Slater.

"We were doing the show at the lot of Desilu/Caheunga and on that lot were a bunch of successful TV series." Schell was in good company during *Gomer Pyle*'s third year. "Along with us on the various soundstages on the lot was *The Dick Van Dyke Show, Make Room for Daddy, I Spy, Hogan's Heroes* ... shows like that." They were all, either directly or indirectly, handled by former movie star and then TV mogul Sheldon Leonard, who more often than not teamed up with his good friends Danny Thomas and Carl Reiner. Schell would be joining the Sheldon Leonard/Danny Thomas dynasty on another of the Desilu/Cahuenga stages when *Good Morning World* entered production.

Photo courtesy CBS/Paramount

In the series ... and real life ...Schell and his alter-ego Larry Clark were carefree bachelors who knew the value of a buck. He wasn't cheap, but very frugal. Baker would often joke about Schell's real-life thriftiness.

"He never picked up a check the whole time we worked together ... my God, he should've been Jewish!" But Baker also had much praise for his co-star, describing him as "funny ... weird at times, but funny and a really nice person."

While the role of David Lewis had aged from the twenty-seven-year-old Ron Rifkin to a thirty-three-year-old Joby Baker, the disc jockey's wife re-

Photo courtesy CBS/Paramount

mained a twenty-something newlywed. Twenty-six-year-old actress Julie Parrish replaced Sharon Farrell as Linda Lewis.

"She had a unique ability to perform 'in the moment" as an actress," Baker recalled of his TV wife. "She helped me out tremendously and she never threw a fit or anything. I bitched about everything, temperamental star that I was, but she was never like me."

Parrish, a native of Kentucky, was born Ruby Joyce Wilbar, and got her big break by winning the national modeling contest "Young Model of the Year" in Tecumseh, Michigan that had Jerry Lewis as its judge. That led to her winning the prize of an appearance in his next film, an uncredited part in the 1962 film *It's Only Money*. But that almost didn't happen. Upon her arrival in Hollywood to claim her grand prize, Lewis' director knew nothing about the contest much less her role in the movie. In the end, he wrote in a small role for her and later she was farmed out to MGM's acting school. When she was cast in his next film, 1963's *The Nutty Professor*, she changed her name to Julie Parrish and had the small role as a college student.

Photo courtesy CBS/Paramount

The film career for the five-foot-five, 106-pound auburn-haired actress with big hazel eyes included another uncredited role in *Harlow* in 1965 to be followed by more recognizable parts in *Winter a Go-Go* that same year and opposite Frankie Avalon in *Fireball 500* in 1966. But it was the 1966 Elvis Presley film *Paradise, Hawaiian Style* that theatregoers remember Parrish best for. In one of the film's best moments, she held a group of dogs at bay while The King sang to her in a helicopter.

Parrish's television career made her a favorite to fans of the small screen. She made her TV debut in a March 1961 episode of *The Untouchables* and appeared throughout the 1960s on Westerns like *Gunsmoke*, *Death Valley Days* and *Bonanza*, crime dramas such as *The F.B.I.* and *Burke's Law*, and on the sitcoms *Family Affair* and *Pistols and Petticoats*. But it was another revamped pilot episode that would enshrine Julie Parrish into television history.

After NBC rejected the first pilot for *Star Trek*, the original episode that starred Jeffrey Hunter as the Enterprise's captain was shelved. Later, NBC wanted to see another pilot episode, which became "Where No Man Has Gone Before." However, during the shows' first season, the first pilot was taken off the shelf and edited into *Star Trek*'s only two-part episode, "The Menagerie." Appearing in the episode as Miss Piper, striking in her red Starfleet miniskirt uniform, was Julie Parrish. She didn't have very many lines but she has a reserved space in the Star Trek Universe parking lot and in any *Star Trek* trivia book.

Before Parrish won the role of Linda Lewis, another actress was being considered. Sam Denoff recalled the day when a slim blonde dancer showed up to audition for the part. She was barely twenty-one years old and a petite five-foot-five and 115 pounds. "An agent from the William Morris office sent over this little blonde girl who was a dancer and had never acted before." Denoff and his partner evaluated her performance and came to the conclusion she was much too young to pull off the role of the wife, being ten years younger than Joby Baker. "We looked at her and said to ourselves, 'Jesus, she's not much of an actress but there's a quality there that we really liked."

Twenty-one-year-old Goldie Hawn brought a cute giddiness, tinged with a hint of innocence, to her audition that day ... in addition to a shopping bag full of props. "This agent from the Morris office had seen her in the *Andy Griffith's Uptown-Downtown Show* TV special and had her come in and audition." Art Simon told Sam Denoff that there was just something about this dancer ... something better. "I remember the audition scene was the wife and a neighbor was having a cup of tea or coffee together ... and in her preparation she brought

Photo courtesy CBS/Paramount

her own teacup … it was so sweet."

Goldie Hawn had been a dancer since the tender age of three and was studying drama when she dropped out of American University to try to break into the entertainment industry, which she did when she was a dancer on the can-can line at the 1965 New York World's Fair. This led to other jobs, mainly as a dancer, but she knew if she was going to get into show business Los Angeles was the place to be. The 1966 *Andy Griffith* special was the right job at the right time.

Later, after the audition, Hawn was informed that she just wasn't right for the part of the wife, but they wanted her for the supporting role of the next-door neighbor who was also the girlfriend of Larry Clark. She was a little confused since she wasn't aware that such a role existed in the new TV series.

"It didn't exist until she came in," Persky said. "After her audition, we created the role of Larry's girlfriend Sandy Kramer just for Goldie."

Good Morning World would be Goldie Hawn's first television series.

For the 1967-68 television season, there were six new situation comedies on the docket. Of all that can be said of that year, at least the producers did attempt to create some new vocations for their characters. On the schedule was a prospector who had been frozen for the last century and came back to life after an avalanche (*The Second Hundred Years*), a nun who could fly (*The Flying Nun*), a nightclub entertainer living on a farm (*Green Acres*), a newspaper cartoonist and his wife (*He & She*), a pair of arguing mothers-in-law (*The Mothers-in-Law*), and the adventures of a pair of Los Angeles radio DJ's (*Good Morning World*). It was hoped that the influx of these varied situations would give the old domestic comedy formula somewhat of a new look.

Everyone except Eve Arden and Kaye Ballard (*The Mothers-in-Law*), Sally Field (*The Flying Nun*), Ronnie Schell (*Gomer Pyle, U.S.M.C*) and to a lesser extent Joby Baker and Julie Parrish (*Good Morning World*), were nearly new to regular TV audiences, which can be a mixed blessing. On one hand it gives the new season a fresh look. On the other, the audience tends to not identify with unfamiliar faces.

This isn't to imply that the stars of these new sitcoms were a bunch of hacks. There was a lot of experienced talent to be found both in front of and behind the camera. However, all the talent that was behind *Good Morning World* or for that matter the other five new sitcoms in 1967 was no guarantee of success. In *Good Morning World*'s case, there were several factors to take into consideration:

- Would the disc jockey gimmick hold the audience's interest? It was new and unique to be sure, and who among us hasn't wondered what those guys we listen to on the radio look like? But would it be enough to grab and hold seven- to ten-million viewers a week?

- How would the personalities of the four co-stars click with the viewers? CBS's rejection of the first pilot was still fresh in memory. The roles had been re-cast ... would the new stars click with each other and the audience?

- If they did click, would there be enough viewers to warrant a series renewal for the 1968-69 season? For all its glitz and glamour, keeping a TV show on the air is basically a numbers game ... you have to reach out, entertain and hold a certain number of viewers every week or you simply don't stay on the air.

- Were the scripts bright enough and was the writing funny enough ... after all, this was a situation comedy. With Persky and Denoff at the helm, and with the likes of Reiner, Thomas and Leonard hovering nearby, this was a minor concern. This team knew what they were doing and had a proven record.

- What about the time slot? Would 9:30 Tuesday nights be conducive to a situation comedy? You can have the best show in television and have the critics applaud it, but if no one watches it ...

- What about the show that preceded it, in *Good Morning World*'s case *The Red Skelton Hour* ... was it strong enough to hold enough viewers so they'd stay tuned to what came on afterwards?

Any one of these factors, or a combination of them, could mean one of two things. Either your show would be picked up when those decisions were made ... usually mid-February ... or you were dead either in mid-season or after a full season run.

In the previous 1966-67 season, there were eleven new situation comedies that debuted in September and of them, only three survived—*The Monkees*, *Family Affair* and the Persky/Denoff creation *That Girl*.

Photo courtesy CBS/Paramount

After approving *Good Morning World*'s second pilot in February 1967, CBS put the new series on the fall schedule for the '67-'68 season. Viewers were already familiar with a sitcom in the 9:30 Tuesday evening time slot since *Petticoat Junction* had been there for the previous three seasons. In fact, the decision seemed to mirror Persky and Denoff's involvement in the highly successful *Dick Van Dyke Show*, which, true to the demands of Proctor & Gamble, had a similar time slot on Wednesday nights following *The Beverly Hillbillies*. To further bolster an already solid lineup, CBS moved the residents of the Shady Rest Motel to the same time Saturday nights, coming on right after Bob Crane's *Hogan's Heroes*.

By mid-March 1967, all three networks had firmed up their fall lineups. While TV audiences readied themselves for a spring and summer of reruns, the various television production companies shifted into high gear as preparations got underway for the next season, which was only four and a half short months away.

Bill Persky and Sam Denoff formed "Discus Productions" and set about the task of scriptwriting and set construction.

It was finally time to get *Good Morning World* on the air.

Chapter 3:

Behind the Scenes

Following approval of the second pilot in February, CBS gave the go-ahead for production to begin on *Good Morning World* in March 1967 with shooting scheduled to begin in July. Unlike television today, the networks used to announce their fall lineups in February, usually close to Washington's Birthday. During the 1960s that date was moved up to March 15. Today, it can be as late as Memorial Day, which means producers and directors, not to mention cast members, are scrambling to get their shows ready for air by mid-September. For the '67-'68 season, Persky and Denoff had plenty of time ... nearly four months ... to write and polish the scripts and thus allow their new series to put its best foot forward when *Good Morning World* debuted on September 5.

Photos courtesy CBS/Paramount

Another plus that removed some of the pressure from the pair of TV producers was that Proctor & Gamble, the primary sponsor of the show, had guaranteed them a twenty-six-episode run, and another twenty-six-week rerun schedule. Persky and Denoff's Discus Productions knew going in how much money was in the budget and how many episodes to produce.

Sam Denoff said it was easier to do a better job back then.

"During those days, show producers had two extra months to get their shows ready to go on the air," he said. "We had time to get a lot of scripts written and get done with all the things that go into getting a show on in time for the fall schedule." Another thing that is different was interference from the network and the control it has today over the final product. "The only people Billy and I had to answer to was the sponsor, Proctor & Gamble … and the censor, who told us we couldn't say things like 'pregnant' or 'diarrhea.'"

It was still hard work getting a show on the air, but not as stressful as it is today. "When we started the show, we had our old mentor Sheldon Leonard, who would come around and help out when needed." Denoff still fondly remembers him as "the smartest guy in the world. And Carl Reiner, our old mentor from the *Van Dyke Show*, would be there, too." Both Denoff and Persky described *Good Morning World* as a 'happy, comfortable set,' which made it fun to come to work and put in those twelve- to fourteen-hour days.

Joby Baker would remember it differently as the season progressed. *Good Morning World* was to be the start of, he hoped, great things to come, but instead saw the beginning of some major problems in this phase of his career.

"He was an improvisational actor before it was called improv," Persky said of Baker. "And he had a *lot* of trouble committing to and remembering dialog. We went through all kinds of stuff with him and he would always be forgetting his lines."

"I was great at ad-libbing, that I had down pat," Baker said of the difficulties in remembering his lines, "but there were several times where they would change the script while I was in makeup, maybe twenty minutes before we went on … pages of copy would be changed and I just couldn't handle it."

"What they didn't know," Baker continued, in describing his acting style, "is that I'm the type of actor who is very good at what he does when I'm into a deep character … that's why we got into the business in the first place, to become someone else."

Ronnie Schell remembered Baker tacking up little notes and scraps of paper around the set out of view of the camera to prompt him when he began to feel the script slipping away. "There was a time on one show where I had my back to the camera and in this particular scene, he had some lines scribbled down and taped to my chest … it was funny at the time, but in looking back it hurt the show."

Baker laughs about it now, but during production he went to extreme measures to keep the dialog going when his memory wasn't. "I used to have them glue stuff onto their foreheads when I was doing close-ups … God, I'm surprised in looking back I got as far as I did!"

Photo courtesy CBS/Paramount

One of Baker's major problems with *Good Morning World* stemmed from a lack of character development from the start. "They wanted me to be 'Joby'... they loved Joby, but as an actor, I didn't know who that was." Adding to all that insecurity was a little known fact of *Good Morning World's* original title.

"When I first got this part, they wanted to call it *The Joby Baker Show* ... in fact, I've still got a ticket stub from CBS that says that on it." Baker related that Proctor & Gamble told Persky and Denoff that they wanted essentially another *Dick Van Dyke* type of show. "When I heard about their plans, I begged them not to call it that because I figured if they did, I'd really be in trouble."

Baker's anxiety wasn't rooted in his doubts as an actor. His abilities combined with some fine tuning of *Good Morning World* would have been more than enough for the series to equal the five-year run of *The Dick Van Dyke Show*. His uncertainty stemmed from the shadow that Van Dyke still cast.

"They thought they had another Dick Van Dyke in Joby Baker," he said. "There *is* no other Dick Van Dyke! When he was born, he came out of the womb and tripped over the doctor, for God's sake!"

He also thought the scripts could have been better... a lot better.

"The reason I had trouble memorizing the lines is they were horrible fucking lines," he said without hesitation. "I mean, if they were really great lines ... really well written, you'd have no trouble remembering them." Throughout the course of the series, Baker thought the scripts were "corny" and the show "not really that funny at times." In all fairness, in looking back on the episodes now that they're on DVD, he was on to something. Some episodes have lines that fall flat and others are simply just not that funny.

"The problem you get with writers of some sitcoms of that era ... *Lucy* writers, *Van Dyke* writers, guys like that," Baker mused, "is that it wasn't a funny show, it was funny lines." In the end run, the lines were entertaining, but not necessarily the show itself, which flew in the face of Baker's correct assessment. "To me, the situation should be funny, not the lines ... I feel really strong about that. Otherwise, instead of a 'situation comedy' you have a sort of 'linear comedy.' Your scripts should be driven by the situation, not the lines you put into the characters' mouths." Baker's frustrations and dissatisfaction with the series would grow in the months ahead.

On the other side of the record was Ronnie Schell who, like Baker, honed his craft doing stand-up comedy in nightclubs. Persky and Denoff had a routine they pulled on Schell in the waning days of *The Dick Van Dyke Show*. The lure would be in making the actor believe that they might have a character he would be right for that week. Persky described the scenario.

"Sam and I would tell him about this character we had in mind for him, only he was English." Immediately, Schell would lapse into a Cockney accent. "But he has a mother who is Chinese so there is still a little of that in him," followed by Schell adding an Asian flair to the character. The ruse continued. "Then Sam would say, 'but he has very short arms' so he has trouble reaching for things," and not missing a beat, Schell would shrug up his shoulders and pull his hands up under his sleeves. "We kept adding characteristics and he kept incorporating them into the very next thing he said so by the time we were done piling up the traits this character had, we had Ronnie crawling on the floor because we told him he had no legs and his nose was pushed in and he was nearsighted as well ... it was hysterical!" No matter how ridiculous the character got, Schell would add it to the list, much to the hilarious laughter coming from the producers and crew.

Unlike motion pictures, where a production may be spread out over several months, performers in a weekly TV series have only a few days to commit their scripts to memory and rehearse their scenes. In *Good Morning World*'s case, this amounted to a performer memorizing pages of new scripts about once every five days. That fact alone nearly drove Baker to drink! After rehearsal and script revisions, what would evolve into a twenty-four-minute show would be performed and filmed before a live studio audience. Ronnie Schell to this day still laughs at his "listen to the master" advice for newcomer Goldie Hawn.

"I was still a little cocky since I had been doing *Gomer Pyle* for three years and thought I knew everything," Schell recalled of the evenings when he and Hawn would rehearse at his apartment almost every night. "Ever the novice, she would want to do the scene one or two times and then move onto another part of the script, not wanting to 'overdo it.' I told her, 'Goldie, for crying out loud, you're never gonna learn unless you watch the master.'"

Schell would go on to advise her that he had been in the business "a long time," so he knew what he was talking about.

"I remember telling her to 'watch and learn from the master.'" Hawn evidently heeded "the master's" advice and later saw her budding career take off like a skyrocket … but we'll save that for later.

Photo courtesy CBS/Paramount

For Billy De Wolfe, a longtime pro with roots deeply planted in the theatre, Joby Bakers' shortcomings in remembering his lines grated on his nerves. "He was the most professional human being in the world and Joby not knowing his dialogue drove him crazy," Persky related of the sixty-year-old actor. "Not knowing your lines was something you just didn't do."

Another thing that aggravated the old veteran was when his fellow actors were late on the set, again, something that just wasn't done in the theatre. While a performer not knowing his lines was an aggravation, being late made him outright furious.

"He used to refer to himself in the third person," Denoff recalled. "'Mr. De Wolfe is getting impatient! You're wasting Mr. Denoff's time and Mr. Persky's money so get here promptly!'" His annoyance carried with it a veiled threat. "If not, Mr. De Wolfe will get in 'Clara Cadillac' and leave!"

"I can still hear him talking about that car of his," Persky said of the car's nickname. "He'd tell us, 'Clara and I are going to Florida …we shall return on Monday.'"

De Wolfe's professionalism … and sense of humor … overshadowed the real or imagined pressures on the set in his nightly phone calls to Ronnie Schell. In the series, their characters would spar like two alley cats, neither really liking nor trusting the other. In real life, they became close friends.

"He used to call me every single night after we worked and review the day," Schell said of the late actor. "He was really hilarious and on the set he used to tell us stories of movies he had been in and the people he'd worked with." At sixty years of age, De Wolfe was balding and wore a toupee, which he referred to as "We never discuss it, Mr. Schell."

"He'd tell me, 'Well, Mr. Schell, I think I'll go get a haircut tomorrow and I don't know if I'll go with it or send it over.'" Schell, ever the antagonist, would chime in "Oh, you mean your toupee?"

A long silence would follow before the voice on the other end of the line would end the conversation with "I said we never discuss it, Mr. Schell, we never discuss it."

Schell laughs when remembering De Wolfe's phone calls. "He was a wonderful man and a real pro. He taught me a lot about double takes and things like that … he was the consummate actor."

Julie Parrish was a serious actress and looked forward to the transition from pilot episode to weekly TV series. Baker remembered working with her as working "with a real person … I mean I was never, ever aware that she was doing the script." He credits her abilities as an actress as not only benefitting the series itself but also in making their scenes together more believable. "She was always so 'there' and so 'real' … I really cared about her." The two became close friends.

In late spring of 1967, in the weeks that followed completion of the second pilot, but prior to shooting the series, the twenty-six-year-old actress suffered a mild stroke. With filming scheduled to begin in early July, Parrish was determined to battle her way back and not allow the condition to affect her career. If any word leaked out that she had had a stroke, she feared she would be replaced on the series. Her secret remained safe but both cast and crew could see that something wasn't quite right.

"There was a major change in her after we did the second pilot," Persky recalled. Sam Denoff added that the stroke hurt her performance at the start of filming. "It

Photo courtesy CBS/Paramount

slowed her down to the point where she was always taking naps while we were rehearsing and whenever she could between takes, but she never told anyone what the hell had happened to her."

A true professional, Parrish didn't allow the effects of the stroke to impair her performance, but Schell described her as "lethargic" and "always tired" through much of the first half of the series. It wouldn't be until early in 1968 that she would even speak about what had happened.

"She took me aside at a party and said there was something on her mind she wanted to tell me about," Denoff said, as Parrish shared with him the details of the stroke and why she may have seemed off her game initially. "It really shocked me since she wasn't even thirty yet."

Years later, Persky would poke fun at her whenever their paths crossed. "Nobody said anything, but while she was recovering from that stroke her memory wasn't anything to write home about. You put her and Joby in a scene together and you didn't know what you'd get!"

That unpredictability would sometimes rear its head on the other side of the stage, notably with the studio audience. *Good Morning World* and its five cousins on the other networks were, after all, situation comedies and that means you have to have happy people laughing during the production. Stand-up comedians like Joby Baker and Ronnie Schell can identify personally with that stomach-knotting feeling one gets when a joke falls flat and the audience just sits there and stares. But sometimes even the best scripts that have the funniest jokes hung on them don't get the smallest chuckle from the audience. That was the case one night when *Good Morning World* had a studio audience that wasn't in any mood to laugh. As it turned out, Sam Denoff was in charge of "warming up" the audience that particular night. It was Denoff's turn to do some "meet and greet" with the studio audience and get them ready for that evening's show. He would go out and talk with the audience, tell some jokes and sometimes do a question-and-answer session, all intended to loosen up the crowd and put them in the right frame of mind for the situation comedy they were about to watch.

An outside company provided the studios with audiences and bused them in for the shows. On this particular night, though, nobody was laughing. Not during the preliminary warm-up session and, worse still, not during the performance of the show itself. This audience was dead and Denoff was almost in a panic until he spotted a familiar figure who was producing another series on an adjoining soundstage next to where *Good Morning World* was being shot.

"I looked over my shoulder through the 'elephant doors' since we were on a little break from shooting and standing there was our landlord at Desilu, Desi Arnaz himself." Denoff was desperate for someone to come to his rescue. "I'm thinking maybe he can save my life here," so he introduced the famed actor to the audience.

"Ladies and gentlemen, would you like to meet one of the great legends of television, and our landlord and one really marvelous guy?" Arnaz heard the introduction from across the soundstage and shrugged his shoulders, giving Denoff an indifferent glance. "Would you please welcome Mr. Desi Arnaz to our stage!" At that point the previously comatose audience came to life into thunderous applause as *I Love Lucy's* ex-husband wandered onto the set of *Good Morning World*. With the audience breaking into wild applause and giving Arnaz a hearty welcome, Denoff breathed a sigh of relief … but not for long.

"He walked out onto the stage and what I didn't know was that he had had about a half a bottle of something by this time, which he was doing a lot of since his divorce from Lucy." With the applause subsiding, the actor took his bows and then told the audience what was on his mind … in no uncertain terms.

The first thing he said was "Listen! Now what the fuck is wrong with you people?" Denoff's jaw dropped almost to the floor as the former Cuban bandleader let loose with remarks inspired by whatever he had been drinking that night. "I mean, this is funny shit here! Now c'mon, you people, wake up out there!" And that's what the audience did. They laughed and applauded Arnaz again as he waved goodbye and returned to his own set before the elephant doors closed.

"Damn, he almost gave me a heart attack that night," Denoff laughed, still filled with admiration years later for their late landlord. "He was a great guy and a genius, and his studio was like a miniature college campus, where Billy and I were being nurtured … it was really a great place to work."

Good Morning World was being produced on the soundstages of Desilu/Cahuenga, which was separate from the main studio at Desilu/Gower. "We were lucky, Persky and I, to have these guys who had worked first in radio and then in television and movies, mentoring us. We were writing for these gray-haired guys and they were teaching us … you just don't see that in the studio's today."

The series, being about a couple of radio disc jockeys, would sometimes feature real-life radio personalities in the episodes. The man responsible for the title of the show, William B. Williams, could often be seen hanging out on the set of his sign-on namesake. Los Angeles DJ Johnny Holliday was cast in the role of a newly hired newscaster in a flashback episode and in his autobiography speaks fondly of his experiences on the set and highly of Ronnie Schell. Schell related about another DJ friend of his that they tried to get in

Photo courtesy CBS/Paramount

front of the camera. "I had a close friend named Don Sherwood, who was the number one morning radio personality from my native San Francisco, and we invited him on the show." Like a lot of radio people who come alive behind the microphone, put them in front of a camera and they freeze right up. Sherwood got cold feet and chickened out prior to shooting. "That would've been a bombastic, highly-rated show for the Bay area, but it never came to pass."

Another episode featured Cincinnati television personality Bob Braun as an emcee for a 'DJ of the Year' awards show. "I met Bob when he came out to do *Good Morning World* and did his show when I was in Cincinnati," Schell remembered. "I'd be on Nick Clooney's show up in Columbus too when I was doing a nightclub in Cincinnati, Dayton or Columbus … they were great guys."

Crosley, then later Avco Broadcasting, was legendary for live local Midwest television programming. Personalities like Paul Dixon ("Paul Baby"), Ruth Lyons ("The 50-50 Club"), Bob Braun, Phil Donahue, Nick Clooney and Dean Richards ("The Midwestern Hayride") were household names throughout the '50s, '60s and '70s. Bob Braun was the only one able to keep live local variety television on the air until his *Braun and Company* was cancelled in 1984. He then moved to California and could be seen in national commercials for a variety of products. In the late 1990s, his health failing, Braun returned to his native Queen City and worked as a radio personality until his death in 2001.

Photo courtesy CBS/Paramount

Still another radio personality found his way into the fictional studio of The Lewis and Clark Show, that being one of the people upon whom the series was based on, New York DJ Gene Klaven. The memories of the old Klaven and Finch show on WNEW were still fresh in the minds of Persky and Denoff so for one episode, they invited their old friend to appear as the stations' alcoholic yet professional newsman Big Jack Jackson. Klaven passed away in the fall of 2004 at the age of 79.

While Baker and Schell's portrayal of radio DJ's Dave Lewis and Larry Clark was right on the mark, their "studio technique" left much to be desired. "When we worked the controls at the panel on the set of the radio station, they were all wrong," Schell laughed, admitting he was never a real-life radio DJ. "We didn't know what we were doing; all we were concerned with was moving our hands and keeping the dialogue moving along … seasoned radio people like you must've thought we were nuts!" Neither actor had the discipline to learn what did what on their fake control board and since the audience didn't know what was going on either, no one was the wiser. "We did learn one thing in doing the show. Before we talked, we were told to flip a switch to turn on the mike, even though you guys that are on the air know full well we couldn't hear ourselves since we rarely put on our headphones."

"Neither one of us ever worked in radio but Ronnie and I did get the chance to do some on air promo stuff at some Los Angeles radio stations," Baker said. By his own admission, neither he nor Schell had the "voice" for radio. "The only way I could ever sound like a DJ was when I did my impressions and made fun of guys like you!"

Even though they had no background in being radio DJ's, Dave Grusin's opening theme for the series painted a realistic portrayal of what it can be like doing a morning show on radio. In typical Grusin style, *Good Morning World's* opening theme was a blend of jazz and pop, upbeat and bright when synced up with the video of rushing to the station and jumping on the air at the last minute. Grusin's composition is interspersed with rapid fire video of an alarm clock going off at 4:30 in the morning, a rushed Joby Baker shaving, getting dressed and driving off before swerving onto a freeway access ramp. The theme music builds with a cascading drum roll to a shot of the sun coming up over the L.A. skyline. Baker quickly emerges through the studio door, checks his watch to see how late he is before quickly flipping a couple of switches, leaning over the console and yelling "Good Morning World!" to his fictitious listeners. As the baseline of the theme establishes, Ronnie Schell rushes in next to him, motioning a guilty "Hi, Mr. Hutton" to Billy De Wolfe, who is giving them both a disgusted look from behind the glass of the engineers' booth. At home, the theme cuts to Julie Parrish, who tunes in the radio at home and rests her chin in her hands admiringly. The theme ends quick 'n cold as a record spins toward us and stops, with "Created by Bill Persky and Sam Denoff" on the label. Grusin's theme music is right on the money and set the tone for the series.

Photo courtesy CBS/Paramount

Every show has to have a gimmick and *Good Morning World* was lucky enough to have two. First, the novelty of the show being about a pair of radio disc jockeys. The second was the use of ring whistles used to end the fictitious Lewis and Clark show.

"We thought we were going to be millionaires with those damn whistles," Persky remembered. "They were going to be the biggest thing in America ... I can still hear those guys blowing them ... wwwweeEEEEEEEEEeeeee ... when the show ended we had like a thousand of those things left over. They're probably still in storage someplace."

All gimmicks aside, any television show that wants to be successful *must* reach out and attract a certain number of viewers every week or it doesn't stay on the air. *Good Morning* World was no exception despite P & G's twenty-six-episode commitment. A program director, who had worked in both radio and television, told me once that "This business is just like big-time wrestling ... only here the blood is real!"

In the final analysis, the success or failure of any series is dependent on the dreaded "R" word—ratings.

"That's all we thought about," Ronnie Schell said regarding what went through his mind as an actor trying to keep his job. "First, we worried about the 'overnights' ... then we'd worry about the weekly ratings that came out on Tuesdays." Sometimes people from CBS would express either congratulations when the ratings looked good or concern if the show got hammered.

"The network would call us, usually the next day, with the good or not so good news," Denoff said, recalling those phone calls when he would either breathe a sigh of relief or feel his stomach start to churn. "And they'd hem and haw around with 'Well, you didn't do as good as we had hoped last night' or something to that effect."

Though both Persky and Denoff described the set as somewhat sedate, the pressure to perform and succeed was taking its toll on Joby Baker. As the star of the series, his character was the most visible and the storylines revolved around him. That added not only the outside pressures every actor will experience but also the tensions building from within to someone who is creative by talent and perfectionist by nature. He was getting increasingly unhappy with how the show was going and that dissatisfaction was causing him to literally "get in his own way."

"I remember one meeting where I got called into their office and they were really pissed at me," Baker said of a particular meeting with Persky and Denoff that carried with it an implied threat. "And they told me if I didn't clean up my act then my character was gonna get hit by a car in the next episode and killed off."

After nearly four decades, the dialogue has obviously faded from memory for good and today, Baker still can't remember any of his lines from the show … except for one. "I remember one sequence where I'm in the kitchen and I'm looking at the stove. The dialogue was built around the old saying 'a watched pot never boils.' And I'm watching this pot on our kitchen set and son of a bitch, the thing started bubbling and I blurted out 'Whaddaya know, a watched pot does boil! … and that's the only line I remember to this day from our twenty-six episodes."

Adding to all the pressure was *Good Morning World's* time slot.

"When you're opposite a movie there is no way to build a loyal audience," said Persky of the 9:30 Tuesday night timeslot, opposite *NBC Tuesday Night at the Movies*. "You're at the mercy of whatever the movie was that night." *Good Morning World* occupied the second half hour of the movie and in Persky's words, "If it was a good movie we never stood a chance … you either tuned out of the movie after the first half hour or you were there for the whole thing." NBC knew if they ran good movies with name stars, the average TV viewer would be hooked until their local eleven o'clock news came on. If it was programmed correctly, the network would own the last half of prime time on Tuesday nights.

Like the other networks, CBS aired a special program the week before the new season was set to debut. Its *Get in the Winner's Circle with CBS* showcased the new shows that would start airing Tuesday, September 5, among them *Good Morning World*. In the special, CBS encouraged viewers to "Say hello to two of radio's zaniest morning DJ's. The comedy spins around the life of one partner, the romances of the other and the short-tempered boss of them both, as Joby Baker, Ronnie Schell, Julie Parrish and Billy De Wolfe say 'Good Morning World!'"

It was a difficult birth, but Persky and Denoff's latest brainchild survived a rejected pilot, Julie Parrish's stroke scare, a *very* wet behind the ears Goldie Hawn and Joby Baker's difficulty coping with the realities of being the star of his own TV series. It was evident, to some of the cast and crew at least, that *Good Morning World's* lead star just seemed to get in his own way.

"I may have put the pressure on myself, but to me, the series wasn't relaxing," he said in retrospect. *Good Morning World* was the only production, movie or TV, where Baker, by his own admission, "got in his own way." "On all of my other shows I felt like if something went wrong, big deal, we'll do it again … not so on *Good Morning World*," and with that came the pressure to succeed … or else.

Whatever Baker's demons were, real or imagined, they would haunt him all through the series.

Chapter 4:

Good Morning World Episode Guide

TV Guide 1967-68 Fall Preview—courtesy TV Guide

Good Morning World was set to occupy the time slot vacated by *Petticoat Junction* in CBS's Tuesday night schedule. America was already used to watching a thirty-minute situation comedy right after *The Red Skelton Hour*, so nine-thirty Tuesday nights was the obvious place for the network to debut its newest sitcom.

ABC would be premiering a police drama entitled *N.Y.P.D.*, while NBC was staying with the tried-and-true *NBC Tuesday Night at the Movies*. *Good Morning World's* competition was impressive, but not formidable.

Ratings information for the twenty-six first-run episodes of the series are courtesy Neilsen Media Research and are used with permission. The numbers reflect a nationwide audience of 56.67 million households that owned TV sets in 1967. Ratings figures, in percentages, reflect how the show performed compared with every household having TV sets. Each ratings point represents 566,700 households. Share percentages, also expressed in percentages, is the most important barometer of the pair and show how *Good Morning World* fared with those households who actually had the set turned on.

Just like in the fictitious radio world of The Lewis and Clark Show, ratings are always a comparison with the overall population, whereas share numbers are a comparison with those who had the radio ... or in this case...television set on.

Throughout this chapter, as we look at the show's individual episodes, we'll also chart how it fared in the Neilsen's.

"Knits to You, Sir"
(Airdate, September 5, 1967)

Listing/photo courtesy TV Guide

At left, Ronnie Schell, Billy De Wolfe and Joby Baker in a scene from the debut episode "Knits to You, Sir."

Guest star Marty Ingels was one half ("Arch Fenster") of the 1962-63 sitcom *I'm Dickens, He's Fenster*. He's also married to *Partridge Family* mom Shirley Jones. Charlie Brill is remembered by Trekkers as undercover Klingon agent Arne Darvin on *Star Trek's* "The Trouble with Tribbles," and also from his appearances on the mid-1970s game show, *Tattletales*, with his wife Mitzi McCall.

Ratings for *Good Morning World's* debut were adequate, but not overly impressive as the new situation comedy barely won its time slot. The graphs throughout this chapter reflect the more important share percentages.

		Rating	Share
#1	*Good Morning World* (CBS)	21.8	33.7
#2	*N.Y.P.D.* (ABC)	21.4	33.1
#3	*Tuesday Night at the Movies* (NBC)	18.6	30.7

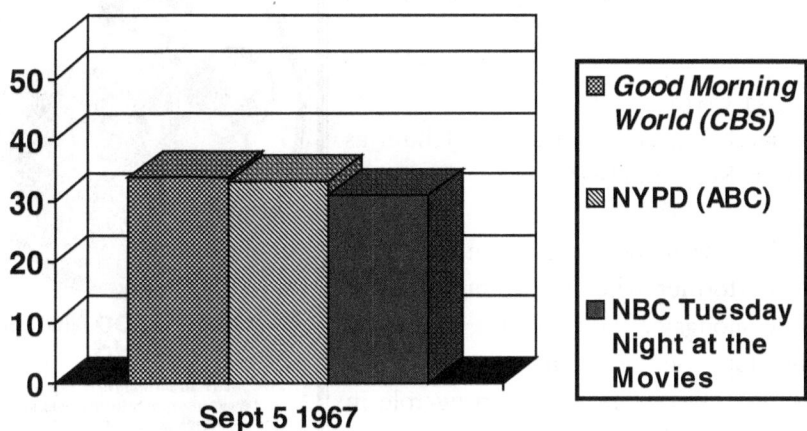

"You Can't Say That About Me"
(Airdate, September 12, 1967)

"Dave's on-the-air jokes about his wife have her fuming, so the deejays conduct a poll to find out what listeners really think of Linda Lewis."

GUEST CAST:
Herb Vigran and David Ketchum as grocers Keith and Bert.

Indiana native Herb Vigran was a radio performer who was in hundreds of shows alongside stars like Jack Benny and Bob Hope long before he got into TV. He was usually cast in a supporting role in various TV shows throughout the fifties and sixties. Vigran died in 1986 of cancer.

His partner in the grocery store scene of this episode was David Ketchum, who viewers will recall as "Murph" on many of the old Union 76 gas station commercials of the seventies and eighties. He was a writer for many series throughout the 1960s and also is remembered as "Agent 13" on *Get Smart!* Look for him later in the season in "No News Like Nude News," only in that episode, he's wearing glasses.

Listing/photo courtesy TV Guide

		Rating	Share
#1	*Tuesday Night at the Movies* (NBC)	25.5	42.6
#2	*Good Morning World* (CBS)	16.5	26.4
#3	*N.Y.P.D.* (ABC)	14.3	22.8

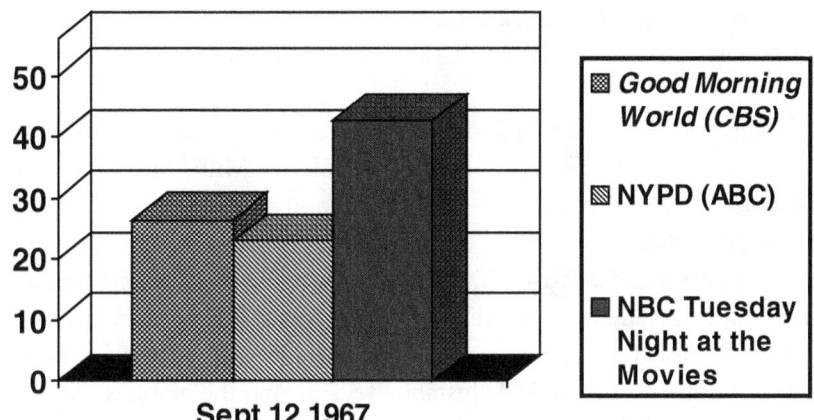

"You vs. Me"
(Airdate, September 19, 1967)

"The partnership and friendship of Lewis and Clark are threatened when both DJs are nominated - individually - for an award."

GUEST CAST:
>   Harriet Hatfield............................ Ann Morgan Guilbert
>   Emcee..Bob Braun

Guilbert has the distinction of having been in the aborted first season of *The Dick Van Dyke Show* in 1961 in the role of "Millie Helper." She is also recognizable from numerous supporting and character roles during the ensuing decades.

Bob Braun had a Top-40 hit with "Till Death Do Us Part" in 1962 and the role in this episode as an emcee fit him perfectly since he was already a regional TV show host and an ex-disc jockey. Nationally, he was familiar as the spokesman for Craft-matic Adjustable Beds during the eighties and nineties. Braun passed away in January 2001 after fighting both Parkinson's Disease and cancer.

		Rating	Share
#1	*Tuesday Night at the Movies* (NBC)	27.4	46.7
#2	*N.Y.P.D* (ABC)	14.7	23.8
#3	*Good Morning World* (CBS)	14.2	23.0

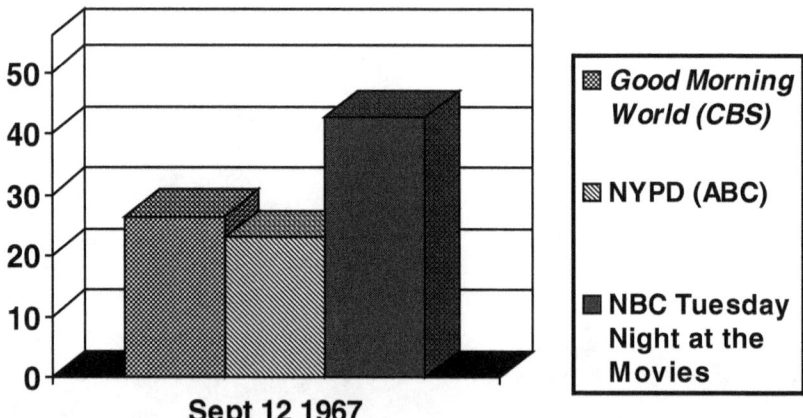

"Love at First Flight"
(Airdate, September 26, 1967)

"Are Larry's days numbered? That's the word he's spreading to retain his bachelor standing - and assure the continuing adulation of girl friend Sandy."

		Rating	Share
#1	*Tuesday Night at the Movies* (NBC)	19.1	33.7
#2	*N.Y.P.D* (ABC)	16.8	27.8
#3	*Good Morning World* (CBS)	16.6	27.4

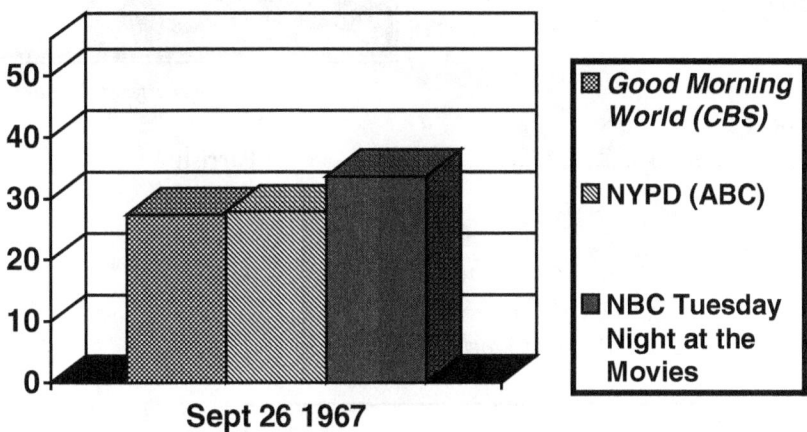

"Buy Calamari"
(Airdate, October 3, 1967)

"Linda runs out of patience when Dave spends too much time with his old sports car—and the lovely young thing who bought it."

At right, Dave and Miss Zelner *after* taking a test drive in his Calamari, much to the chagrin of annoyed wife Linda ...

Photo courtesy CBS/Paramount

GUEST CAST:
Miss Zelner .... Leslie Parrish

		Rating	Share
#1	*Tuesday Night at the Movies* (NBC)	27.7	48.2
#2	*N.Y.P.D* (ABC)	13.1	22.1
#2	*Good Morning World* (CBS)	13.1	22.1

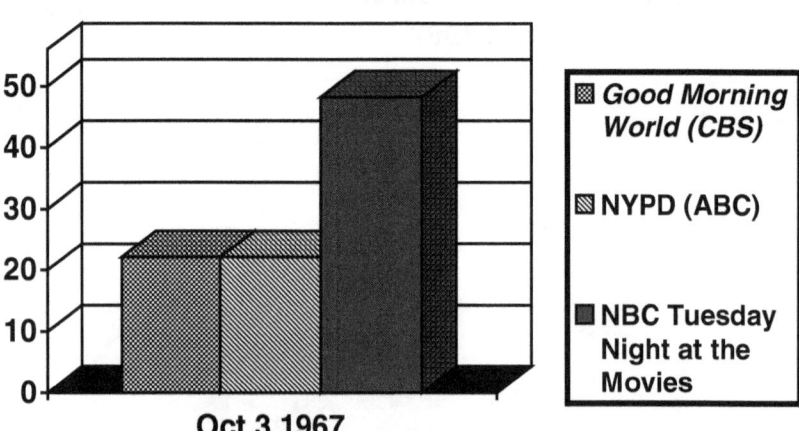

This was one of those rare occasions where second place for the timeslot was deadlocked. One thing was becoming obvious, though, even at this early phase of the season ... *Good Morning World* was being perceived as an under performer, unable to firmly move past *N.Y.P.D.*, and solidly occupy second place on Tuesday nights. It was a foregone conclusion the show wouldn't beat *NBC Tuesday Night at the Movies,* but if it was to survive into the next season, *Good Morning World* would have to start showing it could hold its own.

A couple things of note on this particular episode. First of all, Julie Parrish and Leslie Parrish aren't related. Julie Parrish's birth name was Ruby Joyce Wilbar when she was born in Middlesboro, Kentucky. Leslie Parrish was given the name Margaret Helen when she was born in 1935 in Melrose, Massachusetts and in 1959 changed it to Leslie Parrish. She was one of the first female TV producers and also was a political/social activist during the Vietnam War, in addition to appearing in more than one hundred TV shows throughout the sixties and seventies.

This particular episode was the one featured in the CBS fall preview special "Get in the Winner's Circle," which aired the week before the start of the new season on September 5.

At left, in this scene, Miss Zelner calls David with yet another problem on the car he sold her.

Photo courtesy CBS/Paramount

"Where Have You Gone Billy Boy, Billy Boy"
(Airdate, October 10, 1967)

"While hosting a telethon, the disc jockeys learn a well-kept secret about their stuffy boss: Hutton was once a vaudeville headliner. Billy De Wolfe (Hutton) does a routine with impressions of a chorus line, a snake charmer and a monster."

GUEST CAST:
- Jackie Sullivan .... Paul Gilbert
- Ernie .... A.G. Vitanza
- Congressman Zukor .... Remo Pisani

This was perhaps one of *Good Morning World's* best episodes and a personal favorite of series co-creator Bill Persky, with the writers using some of Billy De Wolfe's life history as the background for a great storyline.

"Persky was Billy De Wolfe's biggest fan and rightly so because he was the best thing that we had going for us," Baker said. "He knew all about Billy's background in show business and was really chomping at the bit to do a performance piece with him."

The plot of this episode dealt with a benefit telethon that Lewis and Clark were hosting, with viewers phoning in pledges in addition to making requests with their pledge. (Check out Gilbert's flip in the opening segment … how he kept from killing himself is amazing!) As the telethon progresses, pledges start coming in for an unknown performer named Billy Jones. Mr. Hutton vehemently refuses to allow Billy Jones to appear on the show and only after Linda gets Dave's book on vaudeville performers do they find out that Billy Jones was none other than Roland B. Hutton in his younger years. De Wolfe's routine near the end of the episode is the stuff that awards are made of.

Prior to being cast in *Good Morning World,* he had been in London for a two-year run in *How to Succeed in Business Without Really Trying.* "Where Have You Gone Billy Boy, Billy Boy" really made use of De Wolfe's extensive career in the musical comedy field.

This episode also contains an oddity in the casting of Paul Gilbert, a veteran comedy actor who had the starring role in the 1954 TV series *The Duke.* He played himself in an entry of the Ed Sullivan Show in 1957 and had several guest appearances on *Rowan & Martin's Laugh-In* from 1968 through its final season in 1973. Among his movie credits, his most noted role was in

1965's *Cat Ballou*. Persky and Denoff caught up with him in a 1964 *Dick Van Dyke Show*.

The oddity is that while *TV Guide* credits him as portraying the role of Jackie Sullivan and while the closing credits list him in the same fashion, Joby Baker calls him by his real name in the episode's opening scenes. Was it a typo, another instance of Baker forgetting his lines or something that slipped by the editors in post-production?

No one seems to know.

Another piece of trivia that figured in the plotline had to do with the mysterious Billy Jones himself. Billy De Wolfe's birth name was in fact William Andrew Jones ... Billy Jones!

		Rating	Share
#1	*Tuesday Night at the Movies* (NBC)	25.1	41.6
#2	*Good Morning World* (CBS)	15.5	24.6
#3	*N.Y.P.D.* (ABC)	15.0	23.8

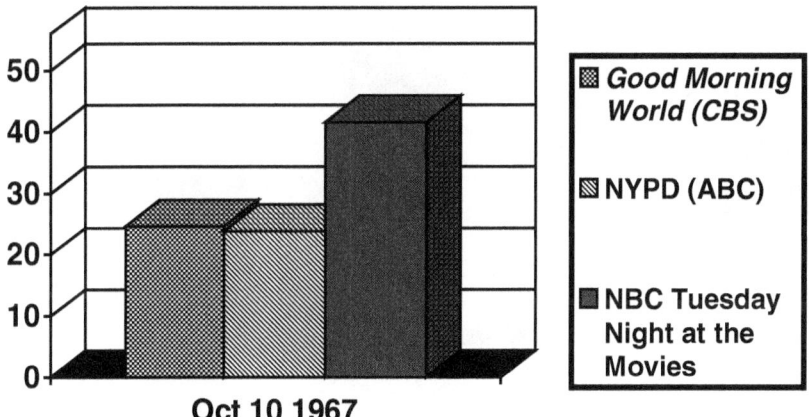

On Tuesday, October 17, the series was pre-empted for a *CBS Playhouse* special entitled "Do Not Go Gentle into That Good Night," starring Shirley Booth and Melvyn Douglas.

However, the other notable event in CBS's new season during this week was its first casualty. *Dundee and the Culhane* had as its storyline a British lawyer trying to bring law and order to the Old West. Series star John Mills found himself and co-star Sean Garrison on the short end of the ratings stick. The show had been going nowhere since its debut September 6 and the network announced it would be replaced on December 27 with a new variety show starring comedian Jonathan Winters. *Dundee and the Culhane* joined the "gone and forgotten" crowd in mid-season after only thirteen episodes.

"If You Go Into the Wild Blue Yonder, I'll Go Wild"
(Airdate, October 24, 1967)

"Dave's desire to take flying lessons gets an emphatic "NO" from wife Linda, so the DJ resorts to rationalization in a scheme to become a flyer—without becoming a liar."

GUEST CAST:
   Big Jack Jackson: Gene Klaven

After seven weeks of Dave Lewis handing off to the stations' newsman, in this week's episode we finally get to meet Big Jack Jackson and it's none other than one of the pair of morning DJ's that the show was patterned after, Gene Klaven of the old Klaven & Finch show from Persky and Denoff's days at WNEW in New York.

He arrived at WNEW in 1952 and teamed up with straight man Dee Finch for the next sixteen years. It not only was the template for *Good Morning World,* but also served as a pattern for morning radio in years to come. Like their counterparts Dave Lewis and Larry Clark, Klaven and Finch improvised and joked their way daily through their four-hour morning show, bringing some wacked out characters along with them.

Photo courtesy CBS/Paramount

Dee Finch retired in 1968 but Klaven continued his morning antics before moving over to WOR-AM nine years later to do afternoons. In 1980 at the age of fifty-six, Klaven said goodbye to radio and moved onto other things such as hosting *America's Movie Classics* and writing a column for *Newsday.*

His "partner in crime," Dee Finch, passed away in 1983. Klaven succumbed to multiple myeloma in 2004 at the age of seventy-nine.

N.Y.P.D was pre-empted for special programming this night, allowing *Good Morning World* one of the few times where it would solidly take over second place on Tuesdays.

		Rating	Share
#1	*Tuesday Night at the Movies* (NBC)	21.1	37.3
#2	*Good Morning World* (CBS)	17.0	28.8
#3	*Armstrong Circle Theatre* (ABC)	14.0	25.5

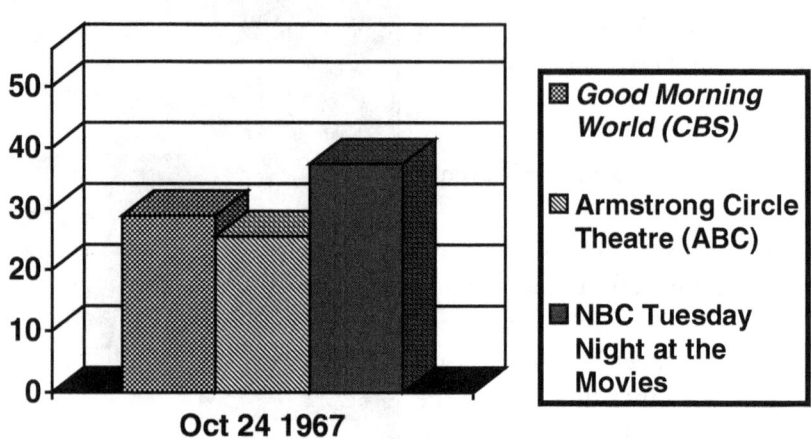

"STAN AND OLLIE MEET LARRY AND DAVE"
(Airdate, October 31, 1967)

"At a benefit auction, a pair of Laurel and Hardy salt & pepper shakers almost comes between the DJ's, who are both longtime fans of the comedy duo. It's up to Linda and Sandy to set things right since each absentmindedly bid on and bought the items, breaking up the set."

		Rating	Share
#1	Tuesday Night at the Movies (NBC)	23.9	43.7
#2	Good Morning World (CBS)	15.0	26.1
#3	N.Y.P.D. (ABC)	12.2	21.2

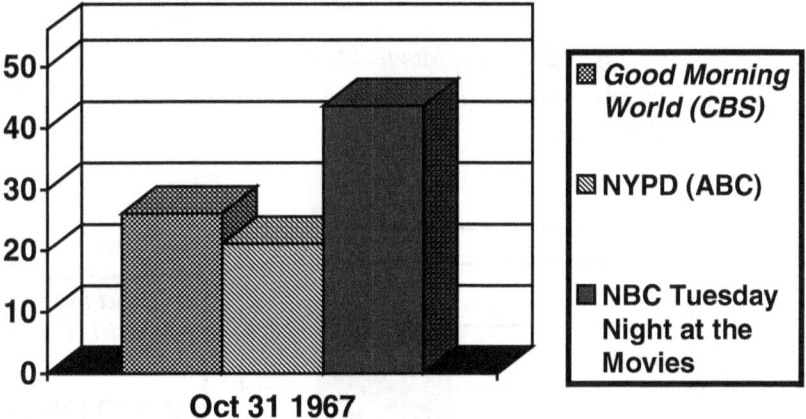

"Feet of Clay and a Head to Match"
(Airdate, November 7, 1967)

"A weekend at Hutton's elegant mansion becomes a nerve-shattering experience for Dave and Linda, who find themselves surrounded by their absent host's priceless—and fragile—antiques."

In this episode, we learn that happily married Dave Lewis is also a pipe smoker and this gets him and Linda into a world of trouble at Hutton's mansion. He breaks what he thinks is an expensive ashtray by tapping his pipe on it. Pipe smokers all across America must have cringed when they saw him holding it by the stem as he rapped on the ashtray ... a definite "no-no" for seasoned pipe aficionados.

		Rating	Share
#1	*Tuesday Night at the Movies* (NBC)	23.1	39.8
#2	*Good Morning World* (CBS)	14.9	24.5
#2	*N.Y.P.D.* (ABC)	14.9	24.5

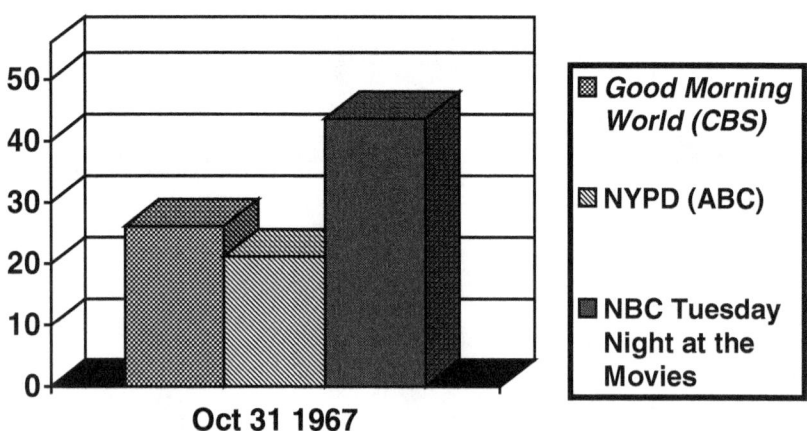

"No News Like Nude News"
(Airdate, November 14, 1967)

"Hutton orders Larry and Dave to do a show from a dude ranch—which turns out to be a nude ranch. Facing the bare facts, Larry and Dave try to make the best of it."

GUEST CAST:
David Ketchum as nudist colony owner Henry Honey

Aside from all the obvious wisecracks about nudism written into the script, the dinner scene with Larry and Dave seated at the Head Table is a joke just waiting to happen. Taking literally the fact that they're at a nudist ranch, they obligingly go to dinner in the nude.

But when the other guests arrive, only Larry and Dave are *au naturale* ... everyone else is dressed for dinner! When you watch this scene, you just know what's going to happen, but you still laugh *at* and *with* their circumstances.

At left is a still from the closing moments of this episode ... Linda greeting her husband in only a bed sheet, seeing as he's just returned after being surrounded by naked women. Do our eyes get to behold the beauty of a young Julie Parrish when the sheet comes off? You'll have to watch the episode ...

Photo courtesy CBS/Paramount

		Rating	Share
#1	*Tuesday Night at the Movies* (NBC)	22.9	39.4
#2	*Good Morning World* (CBS)	16.1	26.6
#3	*N.Y.P.D.* (ABC)	14.1	23.3

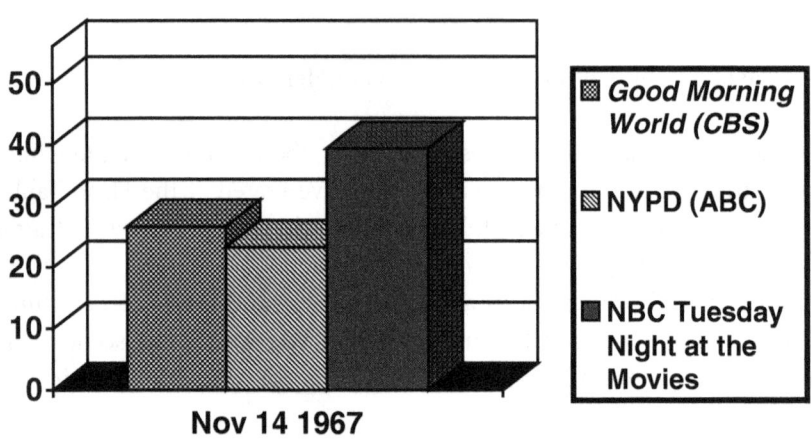

Nov 14 1967

"THE RETURN OF BIBIAN"
(Airdate, November 21, 1967)

"Dave and Linda suffer from a surfeit of niceness as Dave's sickeningly sweet cousin comes for a brief visit - and stays and stays and stays."

GUEST CAST:
    Jackie Joseph as Bibian

Dave's cousin Vivian couldn't pronounce her "V's" so growing up she came to be known as "Bibian" and called her favorite cousin David "Dabid." Jackie Joseph's portrayal of Bibian reminds all of us of that one relative every family has that is so sweet you could just strangle them!

In real life, the talented actress was married to *F-Troop's* Ken Berry ... at least until 1977. After their divorce, feeling alone and betrayed, she became the president and cofounder of "The Ladies Club," which also came to be known as "The Hollywood Dumpettes." It was birthed from Joseph's own painful divorce and became a support and recovery group for the wives of Hollywood stars who found themselves out in the cold, several of them after many years of marriage.

		Rating	Share
#1	*Tuesday Night at the Movies* (NBC)	22.8	39.5
#2	*Good Morning World* (CBS)	18.4	30.8
#3	*N.Y.P.D.* (ABC)	11.7	19.6

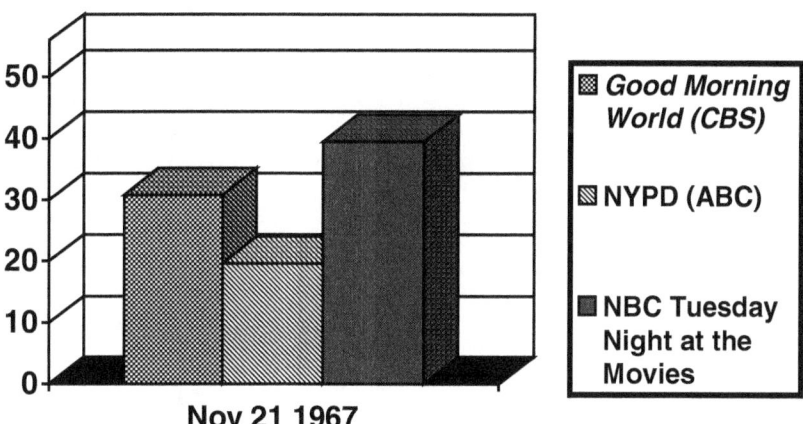

This episode apparently struck a responsive chord with viewers since this was the first time since the series' debut that it scored above a thirty-share.

"If You Marry Me Today, I'll Marry You Tomorrow"
(Airdate, November 28, 1967)

"Dave and Linda's first anniversary celebration prompts a recollection of their Hawaiian wedding day. In a flashback, the couple relive the delays and dilemmas that threatened the ceremony."

GUEST CAST:
  Ace Farber .... Murray Roman
  Dr. Green .... Richmond Shepard
  Linda's Father .... Byron Morrow

Murray Roman, who played the part of the DJ's pilot friend, was a writer for *The Smothers Brothers Comedy Hour* in 1967. He passed away in 1973 at only forty-five years of age.

Among Byron Morrow's many character roles in TV and movies, he portrayed Senator J. William Fulbright in the excellent *ABC Theatre*, "The Missiles of October," in 1974. He was also Admiral Chester Nimitz in the Robert Conrad TV movie *Baa Baa Black Sheep* two years later and played a minister in the 1981 TV movie adaptation of Jacqueline Susann's *Valley of the Dolls*.

		Rating	Share
#1	*Tuesday Night at the Movies* (NBC)	21.3	37
#2	*Good Morning World* (CBS)	16.1	26.7
#3	*N.Y.P.D.* (ABC)	15.3	25.4

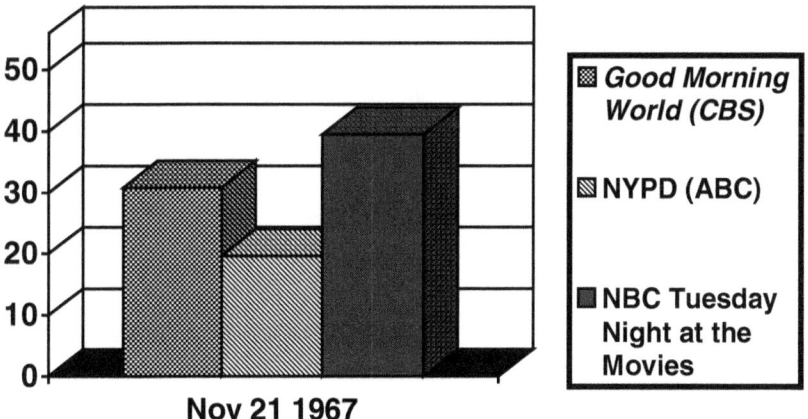

This was a particularly interesting episode in that we get a glimpse into what the characters' lives were like before the big move to Los Angeles and Mr. Hutton's radio station. Both Dave and Larry were bachelors at the time, working for one of Honolulu's smaller stations. Linda was a receptionist at KLUA when she and Dave met and by chance, Mr. Hutton was on vacation there. Like any good radio general manager, he tuned across the dial and "airchecked" the local talent, apparently liking what he heard in the Lewis and Clark Show … and the rest becomes the script line of the series. This is also the only episode where we get to meet Linda's father, who is flown in from Los Angeles covertly to surprise the new bride for her wedding.

"Don't Call Us and We Won't Call You"
(Airdate, December 5, 1967)

"Dave and Larry try to duck out of doing a charity show for Linda's club - then have a change of heart when they learn that some big names are slated for the event. Seen in cameo roles: Andy Griffith and Carl Reiner."

		Rating	Share
#1	*Tuesday Night at the Movies* (NBC)	21.4	36
#2	*Good Morning World* (CBS)	16.2	26.1
#3	*N.Y.P.D.* (ABC)	15.9	25.6

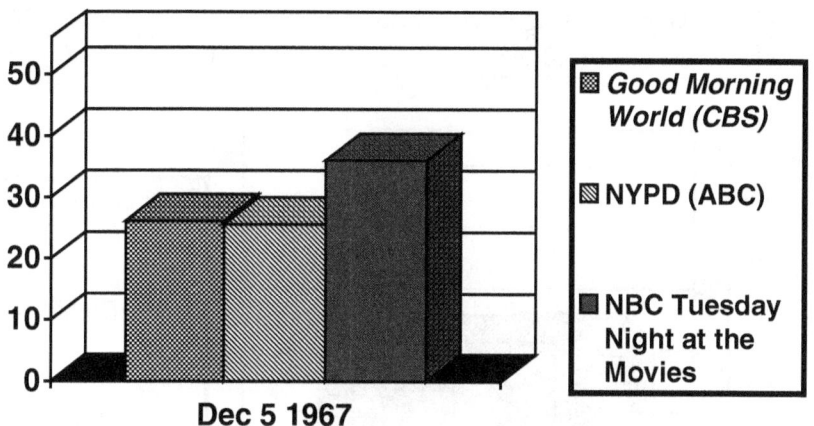

"The Voice of the Turtle is Better Than Mine"
(Airdate, December 12, 1967)

"In a flashback episode, the DJ's relive their first days on the job when Dave's laryngitis spelled near disaster for Lewis and Clark."

Guest Cast:
    Andy McChesney .... Johnny Holliday
    Psychiatrist .... Marc London
    Moving Man .... Don Diamond

		Rating	Share
#1	*Tuesday Night at the Movies* (NBC)	22.7	39.8
#2	*Good Morning World* (CBS)	15.7	26.8
#3	*N.Y.P.D* (ABC)	12.9	22.1

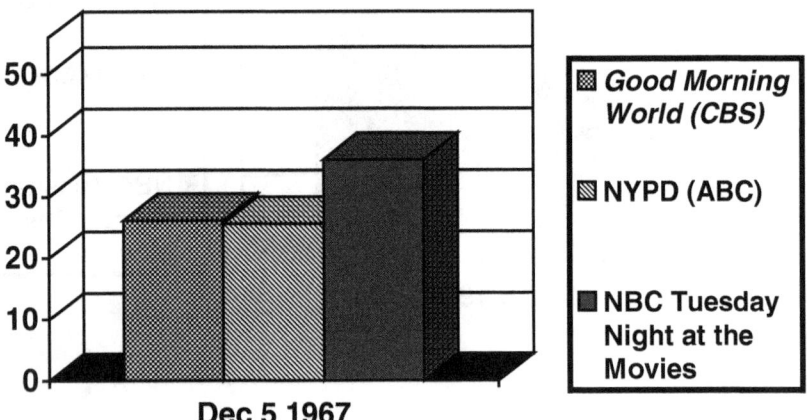

Elements of the second pilot episode were featured in this entry. This was one of a pair of "flashback" *Good Morning Worlds* and for those of us who have ever been on the air, losing your voice is one of our biggest nightmares. Joby Baker does a masterful job of a DJ stricken with laryngitis brought on by the stress and panic of a new job, making this one of the series' funniest and most memorable episodes.

Adding credibility to the episode was the casting of real-life radio deejay Johnny Holliday as one of the station's newscasters. Today he's the veteran voice of the University of Maryland Terrapins football and basketball teams, but back in the sixties he was one of *the* best Top-40 DJ's in the country. Holliday worked in Cleveland, New York, San Francisco and Washington, D.C. and had a lifelong affinity for sports and its heroes. His autobiography, "From Rock to Jock," is a great read ... he speaks highly of Ronnie Schell from this appearance on *Good Morning World.*

Marc London, the psychiatrist who diagnoses Dave with hysterical laryngitis, is known from his supporting roles on several 1960s TV shows and also was a writer for *Rowan & Martin's Laugh-In* and in the mid-seventies for *The Muppet Show.*

The next time you catch a rerun of *F-Troop*, take a good long look at Crazy Cat. Whenever Sgt. O'Roarke and Cpl. Agarn visit the Hekawee's ... that's Don Diamond. He was also a regular in 1951's *The Adventures of Kit Carson* and played Corporal Reyes in Guy Williams' *Zorro* in 1957, but he's always remembered as Chief Wild Eagle's screwball Indian friend.

"The Man Who Came to Din Din"
(Airdate, December 19, 1967)

"After Hutton injures his back in the Lewis home, Dave and Linda bend over backwards to wait on the fussy man, who can't be moved—for several days."

GUEST CAST:
    Dr. Zinnato .... Peter Hobbs

Peter Hobbs has a long track record throughout the sixties, seventies and eighties in supporting roles. You'll see him in multiple episodes of shows like *The FBI*, *Barney Miller*, *The Odd Couple* and *Knots Landing*. His most unusual role, though, came in 1974's *The Nine Lives of Fritz the Cat*. He provided one of the many voices for this first cartoon porn movie.

Photo courtesy CBS/Paramount

No Neilsen ratings were taken this night, however, the scramble for the numbers would resume the day after Christmas.

"Now I Lay Me Down to Sleep, Maybe"
(Airdate, December 26, 1967)

"An emergency forces the DJs to do a late-night show in addition to their early morning stint. The overtime takes its toll on Dave, who can't get any sleep between shows no matter how he tries."

GUEST CAST:
Lieutenant Breitbard .... Ric Roman
Patrolman Nichols .... Geoff Edwards
Fred .... David Astor
Man .... Garry K. Marshall
Agnes .... Kitty Malone

		Rating	Share
#1	*Tuesday Night at the Movies* (NBC)	19	34
#2	*N.Y.P.D.* (ABC)	16	27
#3	*Good Morning World* (CBS)	15.3	26.4

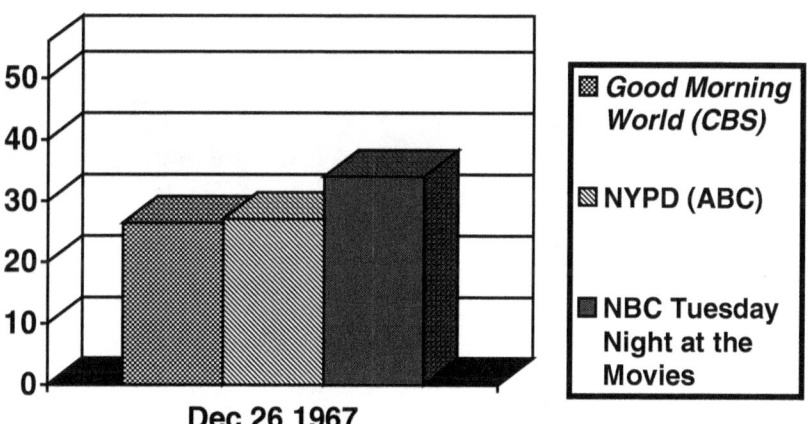

Dec 26 1967

Garry Marshall had a small role in this episode, but was a good friend of Persky and Denoff from their early days writing on *The Dick Van Dyke Show*. It's no surprise after being nurtured by the likes of Danny Thomas, Sheldon Leonard and Carl Reiner that Marshall would go on to be one of the most successful producer/directors in the business, creating and producing such long-running TV hits as *The Odd Couple, Happy Days, Laverne and Shirley* (which starred his sister and topnotch producer in her own right, Penny Marshall) and *Mork and Mindy*.

Geoff Edwards is in the same league as Gene Rayburn, Allen Ludden or Monte Hall. Edwards hosted a string of game shows throughout the seventies and eighties, starting with 1973's *The New Treasure Hunt*. He also hosted a sports show of sorts, the early seventies syndicated *Celebrity Bowling*.

Ric Roman enjoyed a long career in both TV and movies dating back to the early fifties. You'll see him in several episodes of *Zorro, 77 Sunset Strip, Loredo, Batman* and *Mannix*. His most recognizable movie roles were uncredited ones; a Hebrew at Rameses Gate in 1956's *The Ten Commandments* and with Elvis in *King Creole* two years later. Roman passed away in 2000 at the age of 83.

"First Down and 200 Miles To Go"
(Airdate, January 2, 1968)

"'First down and 200 miles to go' pictures the plight of a football fan facing a hometown TV blackout. Determined to see a big game, Dave drives to an out-of-town motel—only to find the TV sets don't work. Frustration mounts as he tries to dash home in time for the replay."

GUEST CAST:
Justice of the Peace .... Robert Donner
Martha .... Mitzi Hoag
Officer .... E. Duke Vincent

		Rating	Share
#1	*Good Morning World* (CBS)	20.4	32.1
#2	*Tuesday Night at the Movies* (NBC)	18.8	30.8
#3	*N.Y.P.D.* (ABC)	16.4	25.8

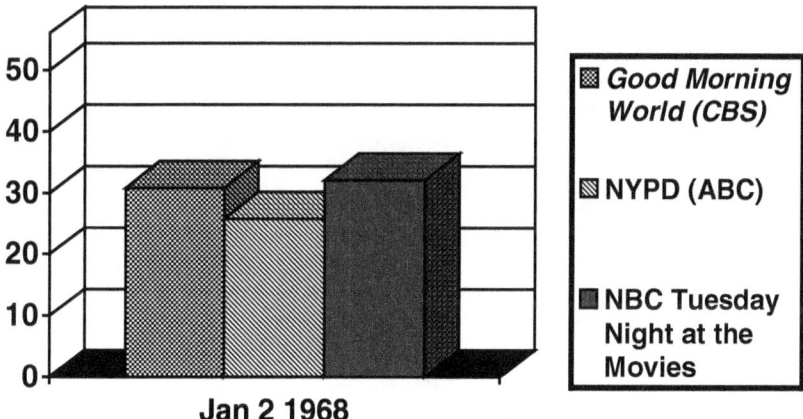

Of all the roles that Robert Donner has played over the years, and there are many to choose from in both TV and movies, he is best remembered as "Exidor" in Robin Williams' *Mork and Mindy*. Others will also recall him as "Yancy" on *The Waltons*. In later years, he enjoyed a string of appearances on *Falcon Crest* and *MacGuyver*.

E. Duke Vincent scored a double header on this episode. Not only did he play the role of the police officer that hauls in Dave, Linda and Sandy for speeding, but he was also this episode's co-writer. Vincent was a story consultant on *Gomer Pyle, U.S.M.C.*, and later went on to writing and supervising producer duties on television and movie productions throughout the following three decades. You see his name in the credits on TV shows like *The Doris Day Show*, *Temperature's Rising*, *The Colbys*, *Charmed*, *7th Heaven* and *Beverly Hills 90210*.

This episode, one of the series' funniest, marked the third and last time it would achieve a share above the thirty threshold. At no other time in the remainder of the season would *Good Morning World* win its time slot.

"I Want a Girl Just Like the Girl that Married Dear Old Dave"
(Airdate, January 9, 1968)

"The Lewises try to help Larry out of a touchy romantic crisis: The bachelor thinks he is in love with his partner's wife."

		Rating	Share
#1	*Tuesday Night at the Movies* (NBC)	28.2	43.1
#2	*It Takes a Thief* (ABC)	23.1	32.2
#3	*Good Morning World* (CBS)	13.8	20

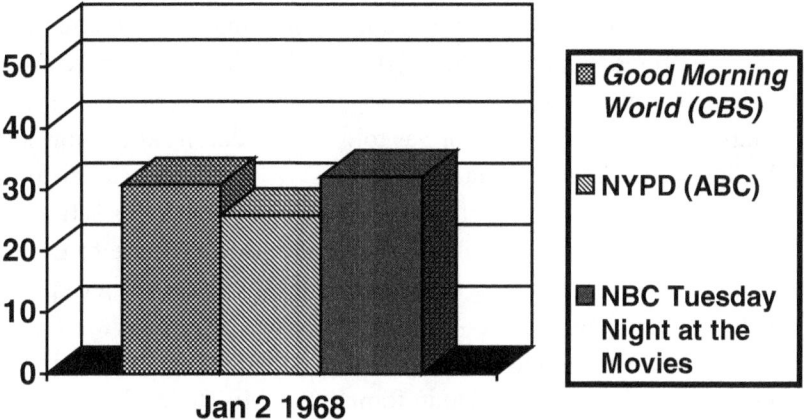

In this week's issue of *TV Guide*, critic Cleveland Amory gave us his two cents worth about *Good Morning World* ...

> "The same group which was responsible for *The Dick Van Duke Show*—Bill Persky, Sam Denoff, Sheldon Leonard and Carl Reiner—worked on this show. But obviously not very hard. Most shows have at least one idea, even if not a very good one. Apparently the idea of this show is not to have any idea at all. Just have five characters in search of an offer. Two of them are men, a radio disc jockey team—one married, of course, and the other not. And, as usual, the big bad boss, the little wife, and finally—who else?— the next-door-neighbor, the girl who's just dying to marry the ... Ah, but we mustn't spoil it for you.

"The show is also billed as having four 'stars'—which really means no stars. The best of them is the 'nice guy' discotalker, Joby Baker, who somehow manages to get some real fun into his role as the happily married David Lewis. As for his harried side-kick, Ronnie Schell, he comes on strong as the bad guy, Larry—you know, the one who is so bone-rotten he wants to stay single, at least for the run of the series. (Our guess is he'll make it in a walk.) Then there's Billy De Wolfe, as the boss, Mr. Hutton, who, as he mugs and shrugs his way through his role, bugs Ronnie for playing so much rock 'n' roll. Finally, there are the girls—Julie Parrish, who gives long shrift to her role as the short-suffering newlywed, and Goldie Hawn (Sandy), who loves Ronnie not just for himself, but for herself too.

"In a typical episode, Larry makes Sandy beneficiary of his airline insurance—something he makes a habit of doing for a lot of girls because he finds that on the next date it makes them very appreciative. When Sandy gets too appreciative, however, he tells her he can't marry her because the doctor has told him he doesn't know how long he has to live. 'The important thing,' he says, 'is to live each day to the hilt—with a smile on your face - like Ben Gazzara.' All this is fine and good fun—until those spoil-sports David and Linda have to make a federal case out of it, and then the show falls flat. Another episode held up a good deal better—in fact, to the end. In this one, Mr. Hutton gets a contract which demands that David and Larry do their program from the Sunshine Dude Ranch. But Mr. Hutton has gotten it wrong—by one letter. It's the Sunshine Nude Ranch. In the best scene, David and Larry finally get up nerve enough to go down to dinner—which they do early so they won't have to enter in front of the others. After they're seated at their table, the others enter—dressed to the hilt.

"All of which proves, we guess, that if you've got no basic idea for your show, then you've at least got to come up each episode with something pretty new and different. To its credit, this show often does. But how much easier it would have been if all those smart fellows had come up with just a little idea to begin with—not a big one, mind you, just a teensy weensy little one."

Of the twenty-six episodes, this was the lowest rated one due largely to NBC's airing of the 1962 movie *That Touch of Mink* starring Cary Grant, Doris Day and Gig Young, and ABC testing the Tuesday night waters with the pilot for the later successful Robert Wagner series *It Takes a Thief*.

"The Wedding Present"
(Airdate, January 16, 1968)

"At long last, Larry makes good on his promise to give the Lewises a wedding gift. But his complicated stipulations send the couple on an embarrassing and harassing foray that hardly seems worth it."

GUEST CAST:
   Uncle Harry .... Herb Edelman

Larry's uncle, Harry Clark, was portrayed by veteran character actor Herb Edelman, who would co-star with Bob Denver in his first post-*Gilligan's Island* series, *The Good Guys,* in the 1968-69 season. You'll recognize him in character roles in many of the comedies and dramas of the period and later. In the 1980s he was a regular in the short-lived *9 to 5,* but enjoyed longer stays in both *The Golden Girls* and *St. Elsewhere.* The tall (6-foot-5), balding actor died in 1996 at the age of sixty-two.

		Rating	Share
#1	*Tuesday Night at the Movies* (NBC)	22.8	37
#2	*N.Y.P.D.* (ABC)	18.8	29.2
#3	*Good Morning World* (CBS)	16.1	25

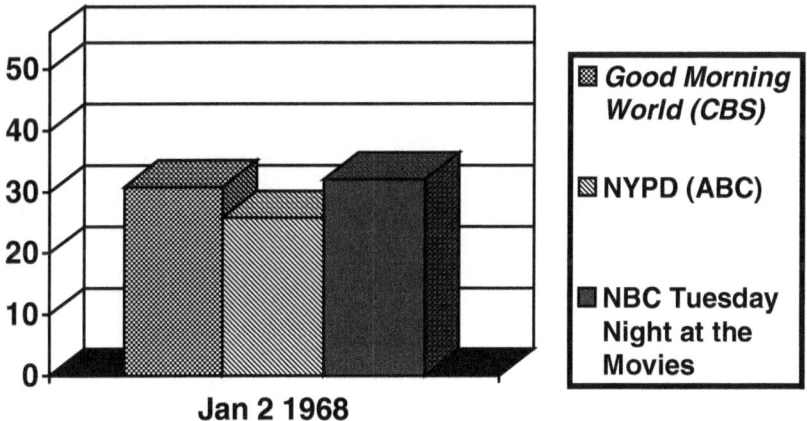

"Partner Meet My Partner"
(Airdate, January 23, 1968)

"Jerry Van Dyke (former star of Accidental Family*) plays Jerry Carroll, a conniving nightclub comic who is scheming to split up the disc jockeys. Jerry's goal: sign Dave as his partner for a new TV show."*

Dick Van Dyke's brother Jerry just couldn't get a decent break. He complained when he was offered the title role in *Gilligan's Island* that it was "the worst thing I had ever read." Instead, he took the starring role of Dave Crabtree in the often maligned *My Mother, The Car.* What followed was a string of flops for the gifted actor and when he was cast in this episode of *Good Morning World*, another in his line of "coulda-shoulda-woulda" beens, *Accidental Family,* had died a quiet death only weeks before. A few years later, the thirteen-episode curse struck again when he was cast in a regular supporting role in 1970's *The Headmaster,* Andy Griffith's first post-Mayberry series. Although he still turned up occasionally in various roles in later years, it wasn't until he was cast as Assistant Coach Luther Van Dam in the Craig T. Nelson sitcom *Coach* that Van Dyke finally hit pay dirt. He's recognizable today for the offbeat commercials he's appeared in for the *Big Lots* chain.

As a side note, after *Good Morning World* went off the air, Jerry Van Dyke was the best man in longtime buddy Ronnie Schell's wedding ceremony.

		Rating	Share
#1	*Tuesday Night at the Movies* (NBC)	26.1	42.7
#2	*Good Morning World* (CBS)	15.3	24
#3	*NBA All-Star Game* (ABC)	13.3	20.7

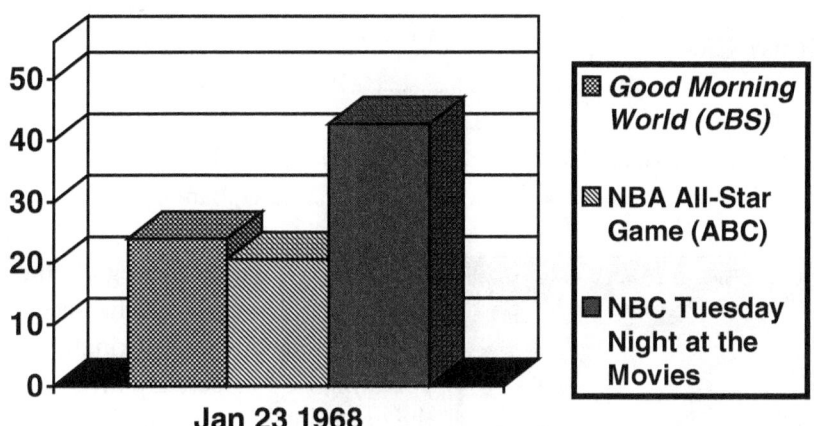

"Pot Luckless"
(Airdate, January 30, 1968)

"Hoping for a big break in TV, Dave and Larry spend an evening at the home of a Hollywood superstar, where they get involved in a high-stakes poker game that could spell disaster."

GUEST CAST:
    Duke Vincent..Pat Harrington
    Jake...Herbie Faye
    John..Johnny Silver
    Billy...Stu Gilliam

Photo courtesy CBS/Paramount

Pat Harrington's alter ego in the early days of his career was his character Guido Panzini, and, due to Harrington's sharp portrayal, he was actually investigated by the government as a possible illegal alien. Harrington's career dates back to Panzini's TV appearances on 1959's *Laugh Line* and *The Steve Allen Show*, where he got acquainted with Persky and Denoff before later reprising the role on *The Jack Paar Show* into the early sixties. He was a regular fixture in movies and TV in the sixties and seventies, even doing voice work in some Saturday morning cartoons. Harrington is probably best known for his character of apartment superintendent Dwayne Schneider on *One Day at a Time* with Bonnie Franklin. You'll also hear him every year around Christmas on the animated *A Garfield Christmas Special* ... he's the voice of John's Dad.

Herbie Faye, who was born in 1899, had a list of TV and movie credits as tall as a skyscraper but is perhaps most familiar to TV viewers as Corporal Sam Fender on the Phil Silvers' *You'll Never Get Rich*, later *The Phil Silvers Show*. His work is a who's who of major TV and movies spanning almost five decades. The eighty-one-year-old veteran passed away in 1980.

You've more than likely heard Stu Gilliam almost as much as you've seen him. He was one of the stable of comedians who called *Rowan & Martin's*

Laugh-In home in the 1969-70 season and had a supporting role in the series *Roll Out* in 1973 as Corporal "Sweet" Williams. Aside from the many supporting movie and TV series roles, like Pat Harrington, Gilliam also made his mark doing voice work in cartoons like *The New Scooby Doo Movies* in 1972 and the voice of Curly Neal in 1970's *The Harlem Globetrotters*. You'll also see him in an assortment of movie comedies throughout the seventies and eighties.

Despite the casting of some great talent, this wasn't one of the funnier *Good Morning Worlds*. For whatever reason, the writing wasn't light and airy but seemed rather tense at times ... not one of the show's better efforts. Despite that, it still managed to win second place this night.

		Rating	Share
#1	*N.Y.P.D* (ABC)	19.9	32.7
#2	*Good Morning World* (CBS)	18.1	29.7
#3	*Tuesday Night at the Movies* (NBC)	15.6	26.3

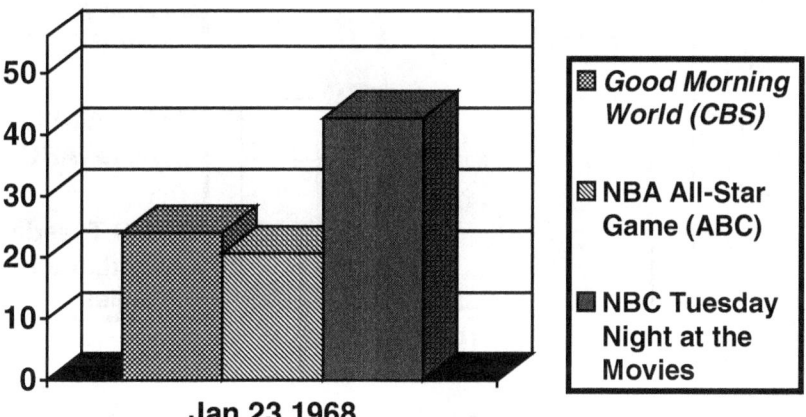

"I Love a Charade"
(Airdate, February 6, 1968)

"Disappointment awaits Dave, who arranged his activities to accommodate a surprise birthday party his wife is planning not to give."

GUEST CAST:
   Judy Cassmore as Christine Andrea

		Rating	Share
#1	*Tuesday Night at the Movies* (NBC)	20.2	35
#2	*N.Y.P.D* (ABC)	17	28.1
#3	*Good Morning World* (CBS)	14.3	23.6

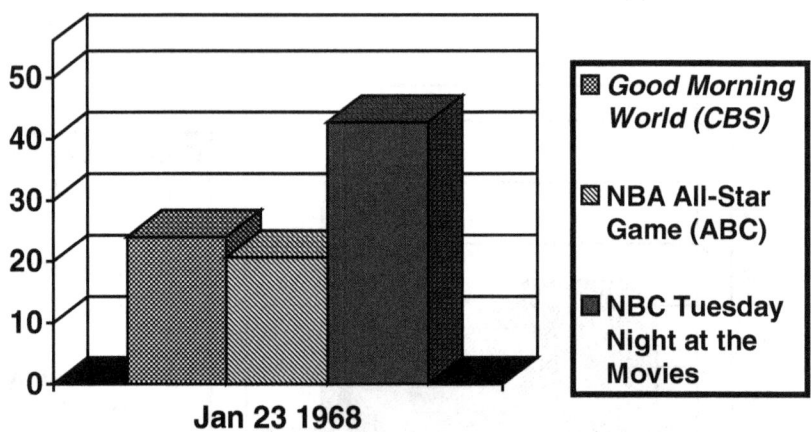

Jan 23 1968

Here's a pair of tidbits from this episode ... both for fans of the show and collectors of TV history. First, this is the only episode that gives Burt Taylor some real on-camera exposure. Taylor played Vinnie, the radio station's engineer, and prior to being cast in that role was one half of the comedy team Taylor and Mitchell. Not much is seen of Taylor after *Good Morning World* and in the years to come, he would become a manager for other Hollywood performers.

The second item of interest is that this is the only episode that still survives to this day in its original form with the network commercials intact. There's a collector of television videos on the Internet that actually has a copy taken from the original 16mm film of what this episode looked like when it ran on the air. It's a hoot to pop in a video tape and hear the announcer crow after the first segment ..."Good Morning World! Brought to you by Scope, the mouthwash that's so powerful, first thing in the morning and your breath feels fresher for hours."

February 13 was another night off for the series as it was pre-empted by a *CBS Playhouse* special, "My Father and My Mother," a drama starring Ralph Bellamy and Jane Wyatt.

However, some trade publications were reporting the possible demise of some shows by spring's end. CBS's Mike Dann described it as "the huge annual chess game" of scheduling the shows for the 1968-69 season. The decision on who goes and who stays would be made in the following two weeks. Several of the shows that survived past Christmas ... *Good Morning World* included ... were still hanging in the balance as of early February.

By this time, CBS was still undecided about some of its shows, while NBC was making considerations of its own. Should Ben Gazarra's character in *Run for Your Life* finally succumb to his terminal illness? Can Major Nelson continue to conceal from NASA that his Jeannie really is a genie? Is it time for agents Robert Culp and Bill Cosby to come in from the cold in *I Spy*? And, lastly, what about the fate of Capt. Kirk and the crew of the Enterprise? NBC couldn't foresee the legendary letter-writing campaign from fans that was on the horizon that would save *Star Trek* for one more season.

With the Vietnam War still escalating and the folks at home growing divided, a comedian once remarked, "If you want to end the war in Vietnam, put it on ABC ... it'll be gone in thirteen weeks!" Over at that network, the list of shows that were teetering on the edge was getting longer. *Peyton Place, The Invaders, The Avengers, The Rat Patrol, Off to See The Wizard, Cowboy in Africa, Garrison's Gorillas, The Second Hundred Years, Batman* ... even the show that was opposite *Good Morning World* ... *N.Y.P.D.* ... were all facing uncertain futures.

By month's end, the winners would be making plans for a new season. The losers ... well, if they were lucky, they might wind up in syndication, but most would just wind up forgotten.

"For My Daughter's Hand You'll Get My Foot"
(Airdate, February 20, 1968)

"Station boss Hutton's animosity toward Larry reaches an all-time high when the bachelor disc jockey falls for Hutton's only daughter, a ravishing jet-setter."

GUEST CAST:
Lynda Day as Cecily Hutton

Lynda Day is best known for her portrayal of IMF agent Lisa Casey in the later seasons of *Mission: Impossible*. She had many guest roles on various TV shows, including future husband Christopher George's *The Immortal*. Four years before in 1966, she appeared with George in the movie *The Gentle Rain*, but it wasn't until after wrapping up filming on 1970's *Chisum* that the couple was married. For the next thirteen years they were inseparable. Sadly, after filming the 1983 horror film *Mortuary*, Christopher George died of a heart attack at age fifty-two. She appeared in a few more productions after his death but the grief was too much and she eventually gave up performing.

Life does go on and she has since remarried and lives in California.

Look closely when Baker and De Wolfe appear in a scene together throughout the series and you might catch an inside joke unique to these two. "I don't know if you can see it on the screen, but he used to talk to me … right on camera," Baker remarked about this particular episode. "He'd whisper to me, right out loud and we had this thing going all during the run of the show." This episode's opening scene has Dave and Larry in the radio studio getting ready to go on the air early one morning when Dave sees this gorgeous young woman asleep on a couch under the control room window, wearing a miniskirt and covered with a fur coat.

"Now we're standing there in front of the couch, on the air, cameras rolling in full view of the studio audience and under his breath I hear 'Mr. Baker?'" Joby knows from prior shows that De Wolfe is trying another of his "gotchas."

"I tell him, 'yes?'"

"I see hairs …"

"You know that would make most people break up but I was so used to it by then," Baker laughed. "God, he was amazing!"

		Rating	Share
#1	*Tuesday Night at the Movies* (NBC)	24.2	40.4
#2	*N.Y.P.D* (ABC)	15.1	24.2
#3	*Good Morning World* (CBS)	13.1	21

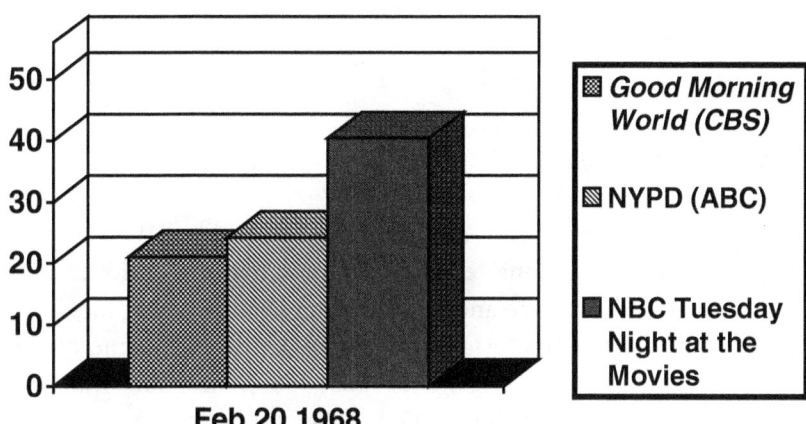

By this point in the season, the Neilsen ratings race was for the most part over and network execs had decided who would stay and who would go. One of the bigger surprises that came out of the January Neilsen numbers was the veteran Western *Gunsmoke,* which was on the verge of cancellation the previous season, now second only to *The Lucy Show* in popularity. On the other hand, the perennial *Bonanza* had slipped down to 24th place behind another Western drama, *The Virginian.*

Would CBS, in surveying *Good Morning World's* numbers, consider giving the Lewis and Clark Show another chance to find its audience, like NBC had done with *Gunsmoke*?

We would know in a couple of weeks when the networks made their formal announcements as to the makeup of the 1968-69 season.

"Here Comes The Bribe"
(Airdate, February 27, 1968)

"Comic Jan Murray plays Mickey Mouze, a pushy record promoter with the gift of gab—and a grab bag of payola. For the benefit of a Government investigator, DJs Dave and Larry recount how they nearly fell victim to the payoff practitioner."

GUEST CAST:
Edgar "Mickey" Mouze .... Jan Murray
Mr. Benson .... George Tyne

Veteran comic Jan Murray, born Murray Janowski in 1917, is best known as a game show host and master of ceremonies. But in World War II, he entertained the troops at home and abroad in the USO. Breaking into TV in the 1950s, he became the first established comedian to host some of the medium's first game shows like *Songs for Sale* (1950), *Meet Your Match* (1953) and the perennial *Treasure Hunt* (1956). Murray was seen frequently in guest roles such as this episode of *Good Morning World* throughout the sixties, along with slapstick portrayals in motion pictures. He also was a regular on Peter Marshall's *The Hollywood Squares* in the late sixties and early seventies.

His most recognizable performance for "younger" audiences was as "The Nothing Vendor" in Mel Brooks *History of the World - Part 1* in 1981.

George Tyne, who played the investigator from the FCC in this episode, was mainly a director of TV shows throughout the sixties, seventies and eighties. Early in his career he was credited as Buddy Yarus.

This episode dealt with the problem of "payola" and "plugola" in the radio business and took a fairly light approach to the situation. For a more realistic portrayal, check out how *WKRP in Cincinnati* depicted the problem when it was on the air ten years later.

		Rating	Share
#1	*N.Y.P.D* (ABC)	18.2	30.3
#2	*Tuesday Night at the Movies* (NBC)	15.4	27.1
#3	*Good Morning World* (CBS)	15.8	26.3

Feb 20 1968

- Good Morning World (CBS)
- NYPD (ABC)
- NBC Tuesday Night at the Movies

The Lewis and Clark Show had the night off for the first week in March 1968, being pre-empted on March 5 by a special entitled *S. Horok Presents*, a tribute to famed impresario Sol Horok. The ninety-minute special bumped both *Good Morning World* and *The CBS News Hour* this week.

However, as described in the March 2, 1968 edition of *TV Guide*, the show was already dead. By mid-February, the networks had firmed up their programming for the 1968-69 season. In *TV Guide's* "The Doan Report," Richard Doan wrote that CBS, enjoying great ratings this season, would be making minimal changes in its lineup. The network would be adding three new situation comedies, a crime drama and a Western to the primetime schedule.

The Doris Day Show, Blondie and *The Good Guys* would be the new sitcoms; a crime drama that would spawn a household catch phrase ("Book'em, Danno!") called *Hawaii Five-O* would debut in September, and Andrew Duggan would star in the Western series *Lancer*. The image of small-town USA would still be around for the '68-'69 season, even though Andy Griffith's character packed it up to become a postal inspector in Cleveland. Ken Berry would star in the re-tooled *Mayberry, R.F.D.*, along with other regulars from Mayberry. But there were four shows that were gone from the fall lineup: *Lost in Space, Cimarron Strip, He & She ... and Good Morning World.*

It's always been said in the radio business that you're not really a member of this industry until you've been fired. By early March 1968, Dave Lewis and Larry Clark had officially joined me in the brotherhood. For Joby Baker, Ronnie Schell, Julie Parrish and Billy De Wolfe, it was time to wrap up any remaining loose ends on the series and move on.

Good Morning World had been cancelled.

"Hutton's Mutt"
(Airdate, March 12, 1968)

"Dave and Linda get roped into caring for Hutton's poodle, a prize show dog requiring meticulous care. Unleashed havoc ensues when the pooch runs away."

GUEST CAST:
  Dr. Crandell..Leonid Kinskey
  Fifi.. Bella Bruck

If there was ever a need for an actor who could put a foreign flavor to his delivery, chances are they would call Leonid Kinskey's agent. You'll recognize this actor from many guest appearances in movies dating back to the early thirties and in later TV shows. Born in St. Petersburg, Russia back in 1903, the veteran performer died of complications from a stroke in 1988.

Bella Bruck was in Neil Simon's *The Cheap Detective* (1978) and in 1976's *Lorenzo and Henrietta Music Show*. (Lorenzo Music was the voice of "Garfield" in that lovable cat's TV specials.) That's just a couple of the roles from her resume, which dates to the early sixties. Bruck passed away in 1982 at the age of sixty nine.

		Rating	Share
#1	*N.Y.P.D* (ABC)	19.5	31.1
#2	*Good Morning World* (CBS)	17.8	28.3
#3	*Tuesday Night at the Movies* (NBC)	18.1	26.7

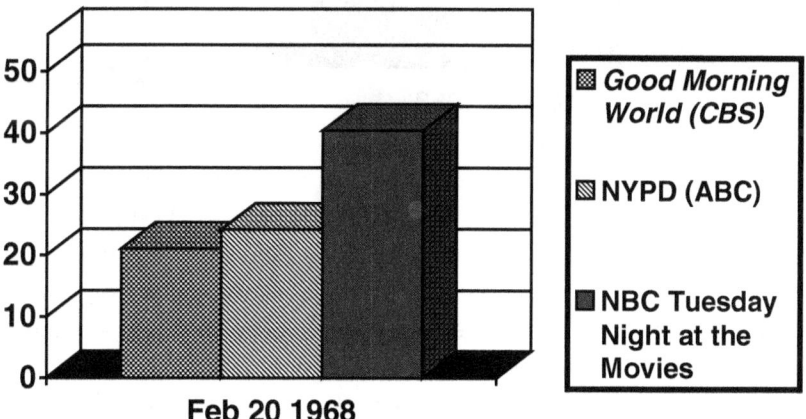

"The Lady and The Pussycat"
(Airdate, March 19, 1968)

"The Lewises get involved in the romantic dilemma of Dave's widowed father. The gentleman, who wants to remarry, asks the couple to help him decide between fun-loving Genevieve or chic Mary Margaret."

GUEST CAST:
- Harry Lewis .... Simon Oakland
- Mary Margaret .... Jayne Meadows
- Genevieve .... E.J. Peaker
- Reporter .... Don Billet

		Rating	Share
#1	*Tuesday Night at the Movies* (NBC)	19.8	34.8
#2	*N.Y.P.D* (ABC)	17.4	29.3
#3	*Good Morning World* (CBS)	15.5	26.1

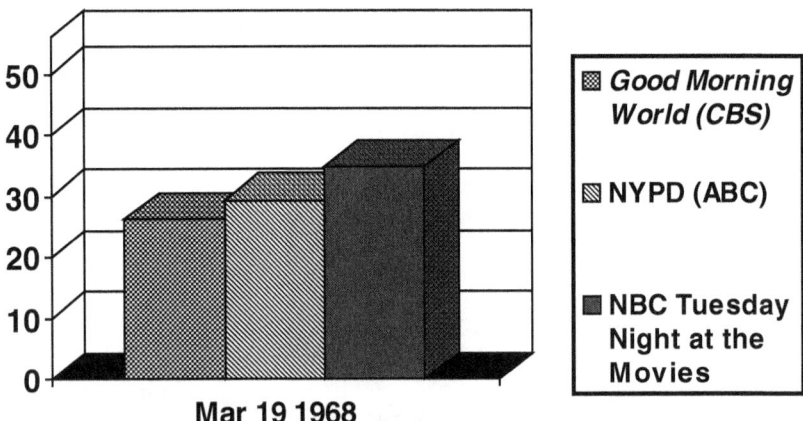

The actor who played Dave's father, Harry, was better known as a tough guy in both movies and TV. Simon Oakland is probably best remembered as Darren McGavin's gruff and frustrated boss Tony Vincenzo in the 1974-75 TV series *Kolchak: The Night Stalker* ... a role he originated two years earlier in the highly-rated "ABC Movie of the Week," *The Night Stalker* and 1973's *The Night Strangler*. His movie roles are a signature of the period; *The Brothers Karamasov, Psycho, West Side Story, The Sand Pebbles* and *Bullitt*, both with Steve McQueen, the two *Night Stalker* movies with Darren McGavin and much, much more. His list of television credits is just as impressive, starting in 1956 with *The Alcoa Hour* and *Gunsmoke* and practically every sit-com, Western, crime-war-medical drama, and late night variety show you can name in the fifties, sixties and seventies.

The tough guy image remained intact throughout his life and into death. Oakland, fighting a losing war with cancer, didn't go down without a fight … the final battle being fought the day after his birthday in 1983. Simon Oakland was sixty-eight.

Jayne Meadows was born Jayne Cotter in 1920, one of four children of American missionaries to China. Most people remember her for her many appearances as a panelist on game shows like *I've Got a Secret*, *What's My Line?* and *To Tell the Truth*. Her movie career after World War II never really took off, but she shined in her many roles on the small screen of television, eventually marrying comedian/actor Steve Allen in 1954. Throughout their forty-six years of marriage, she was also his creative and business partner until Allen's death in 2000.

The perky little blonde in this episode was E.J. ("Edra Jean") Peaker, best known for her portrayal of "Minnie Fay" in 1969's *Hello, Dolly!* Among her TV guest roles, she turned up in several episodes of the early seventies ABC anthology comedy series, *Love, American Style*.

This was to be the last week of *Good Morning World's* first-run episodes. The following Tuesday, March 26, would mark the start of CBS's rerun season. Though the series was now officially out of production and cancelled, it would remain in reruns throughout the coming months before officially ending on Tuesday night, September 17, 1968. CBS began the rerun season with a repeat of "Love at First Flight," which originally aired back on September 26.

Listing courtesy TV Guide

Chapter 5:

"Cancellation *REALLY* Wasn't That Bad a Deal After All..."

"You know you're in trouble when you start hearing people say things like 'What can we do to save the show?'"

That comment, from *Good Morning World's* co-star Ronnie Schell, typified what many were beginning to suspect ... that the series was teetering dangerously on the edge of the cliff that led to cancellation.

"When you start hearing things like that around the set, you begin to think you're not long for this world." Schell began to feel like things were starting to unravel around the nineteenth or twentieth episode. "But we had a good feeling among us ... those of us in the cast ... that things would work out and we'd be picked up for a second season."

Photo courtesy CBS/Paramount

Ronnie Schell's manager was Dick Linke, who was out and about the studio much of the time since he was also an associate producer on *The Andy Griffith Show*. In that position he was more privy to the "in's" of what was going on around the lot and what was happening on the other shows in production. It was Linke who clued *Good Morning World's* co-star in that he might want to update his resume. "Dick called me up one day and asked me, 'Would you like to go back to *Gomer Pyle?*'"

Schell took the cancellation in stride and, by his own admission, was always in a state of anxiety about it. "I was prepared for it," he confessed, joking about it in hindsight. "The upside of being a pessimist is that when bad news hits you, you're ready for it." But the cancellation of *Good Morning World* hurt him deep down. When he speaks of it today, the stand-up comedian inside him kicks in even though the disappointment still comes through. "I never really had any ambitions of being a big star ... I just wanted to work," he said thoughtfully. Then comes the punch line.

"And I guess my career has proved just that!"

The fact that he could go back to his old gang at *Gomer Pyle* with his head held high made the cancellation of *Good Morning World* a lot easier to take.

For Sam Denoff, the end wasn't apparent until the network made the official announcement. "You just never knew," he remembered about the cancellation notice, comparing what CBS would do to mind reading. "It could've been the ratings, lack of support from the sponsor, someone in the network who just didn't like the show ... get into the minds of those people, who knows what you'll find."

Bill Persky began getting that sinking feeling earlier than anybody ... about midway through the season. While the show was a team effort with his partner Sam Denoff, Persky was more in-tune with the intricate day-to-day details and by December 1967 he was feeling like their brainchild was on a slow boat to nowhere.

He was also having to deal with the fact that one of his stars just wasn't working out and unlike a baseball team, there wasn't anybody in the bullpen to go to save the game. "We began to realize about halfway through that Joby just wasn't going to take off," Persky related. "And as good as Goldie was, she wasn't what the show was all about."

Hawn was already making plans to join George Schlatter in a supporting role in his new hit *Rowan & Martin's Laugh-In* over at NBC. "George came over to see us when he was casting *Laugh-In* and that's when he first saw Goldie," Persky said. "Goldie was amazing ... he liked her so much on our show that he signed her right there." No one could imagine how bright her star would shine in the years to come ... no one but perhaps Goldie herself.

"I think she was on a mission ... a Goldie Hawn star mission," related Joby Baker about the actress. "She never really 'hung out' with the rest of us, except for those times with Ronnie." Hawn was always ready and prepared, and "unlike me, always knew her lines." Baker also added the "dumb, ditzy blonde" role she played was nothing like the Goldie Hawn he knew and worked with. "Goldie was on a Goldie mission ... that girl was smart and it really paid off for her."

In hindsight, Baker suspected that while on screen she may have seemed like she didn't have a clue as to what was going on, in real life she was carefully planning her next career move. "She was one of those people who I believe was born to be a star." Goldie, Baker believed, possessed all those qualities that separate "stars" from the rest of us. "She was different, she was cute, she was original and she was very recognizable ... you take a person like that who is so unique, put her in a movie or TV show where people have never seen her and they're gonna fall in love with her immediately."

Contrasting Goldie Hawn's rising star was the growing discontent of Joby Baker.

Photo courtesy CBS/Paramount

"He just wasn't enjoying it," Persky remembered of *Good Morning World's* leading man. "It was probably the pressures of being the star in your first TV series, watching the show not going in the direction that you had hoped it would go … and that problem he had of remembering his lines just did him in." Regardless of the reasons, Baker wasn't a happy camper and told the powers-that-be at mid-season that if by some stroke of luck *Good Morning World* was renewed for another year, he wouldn't be around for it.

"A lot of guys can't remember lines but that doesn't mean they can't do their jobs," Baker said of the recurring problem he had. "I wasn't happy with how the show was being run and the direction it was headed and I wasn't coming back if there was another season."

One of Baker's complaints had to do with not only the lack of apparent comedy in the scripts but also the high esteem those scripts seemed to enjoy. "I remember they would pick over a line … over and over these guys would go … 'should he say it this way or that way' … you'd think this was Shakespeare or something!" The micro-managing of how the actors delivered their lines contributed, in Baker's view, to a tense and anxious atmosphere on the set. "Tell the story and let your people come through for you," he advised.

Another thing that incensed Baker was the strict interpretation of the scripts. While the writer in him understood full well Persky and Denoff's paternal feelings of what was written, the performer in him knew that while the lines were important, the actor had to come across as natural. In his interpretation of what Dave Lewis was saying, Baker had to have the freedom to make those lines his own. "If it's supposed to come out of your mouth naturally, you can't just recite what they wrote," Baker surmised. "Sometimes I would change the lines a little to suit my own personality and they'd blow up and really get angry with me."

In the real world when things are going good and the money's coming in, the workplace has a relaxed and fun tone about it. But when things aren't going so well, the atmosphere gets edgy and tense at the drop of a hat. As art sometimes imitates life, such became the environment on the soundstage of *Good Morning World*.

"I'd walk onto the set and people would be so fucking petty," Baker recalled. "They'd be so nervous about all kinds of shit and I'm just not that kind of guy." Baker admits that it really wasn't anyone's fault in particular, but stemmed from an atmosphere that sometimes establishes itself in the workplace. He described it as a "chicken-shit fear ... and you just get caught up in it."

Baker told Persky and Denoff in no uncertain terms that he was through with *Good Morning World* when the season ended, renewal or not. Faced with the prospect of losing the show's main star and still somewhat optimistic that it would be picked up for another season, *Good Morning World's* creators began to put "Plan B" into effect if it was needed ... a replacement for Joby Baker.

Although they never approached his agent, Persky and Denoff were prepared to offer the role to Bill Bixby, who had come off a successful three-year run on *My Favorite Martian*. If *Good Morning World* were to have a second season, the first episode would have aired on September 7, 1968.

Prior to the start of the fifth season of *Bewitched* in 1969, series co-star Dick York had to leave the show due to health reasons. Undaunted, the producers of the series hired Dick Sargent as his replacement and continued on as if nothing had changed. In the case of *Good Morning World*, Persky and Denoff had no intention of pulling off a *Bewitched*. The first show of the new season would be a clean break and in essence "don't let the door hit you on your way out."

"We would've had Joby's character get a job elsewhere in a big, sad

Photo courtesy CBS/Paramount

break-up episode," Persky said of the never produced season opener. "Then we'd have the new partner come in and take it from there." Bixby's role was never developed but would have been the sidekick to Ronnie Schell's character, with Schell moving into the seat vacated by Joby Baker as *Good Morning World*'s leading star. Baker's departure would also have had obvious implications for Julie Parrish. What little character development there was had Bixby's character happily married to offset the bachelor that Schell portrayed. With Baker's role of Dave Lewis out of the picture, Parrish's role as his wife Linda would be gone as well. A replacement girlfriend for Schell's Larry Clark would have to be found, too, since Goldie Hawn had already signed her name on the dotted line to appear in *Laugh-In*. If *Good Morning World* had been around for a second season in the fall of 1968, half of the regular faces viewers were used to would be gone and that usually doesn't bode well for a TV series.

So what happened? Why does a show like *Good Morning World* that has all the know-how and creativity behind it that a series could possibly ask for go for one season and then disappear into oblivion? Joby Baker credits its failure due to storylines that in his view weren't that funny for a situation comedy, a lack of character development that clued the performers in as to whom they were and micro-management on the part of the producers and the studio, which made life, at least for him, uncomfortable.

His co-star, Ronnie Schell, places most of the blame to the night the show was on. "It wasn't the writing, it wasn't the acting, it wasn't the comedy ... it was the time slot."

Sam Denoff agreed. "The time slot's the whole thing," he said, going on to share what happened six years later when another creation of his fell victim to the network schedule. *Big Eddie* debuted on CBS in August 1973 and starred his old friend Sheldon Leonard. "Because Sheldon was so well known, they decided to start us out early on." Denoff added the new show was in a good time slot and was initially doing fantastic. "Sheldon was thrilled and his wife was so happy ... 'My Lenny is gonna be a big star actor again,' she would say, and she was so proud of him."

Big Eddie was doing so well that when it came time for the networks to shuffle their fall lineups, CBS put it opposite NBC's *Sanford and Son*, which became an even bigger hit in its debut season. Thirteen weeks later, *Big Eddie* was gone, the victim of the dreaded time slot monster.

It was the time slot that nearly aborted *The Dick Van Dyke Show* seven years earlier. The story of Reiner and Leonard pleading their case to Proctor & Gamble is legendary. But the eleventh-hour trip to the sponsor didn't happen in *Good Morning World's* case. While there may have been discussions with both the network and the sponsor … so much time has passed that neither Persky nor Denoff can remember … the plug was pulled and another series was scheduled to replace it.

Why no Herculean effort to save *Good Morning World?* Things had changed from 1961 to 1968. America had lost its innocence in those seven years and television along with it. We had been through the assassination of President Kennedy, growing division at home over an increasingly unpopular war, civil unrest and cities aflame due to rioting over both civil rights and the Vietnam War, and during 1968 another pair of assassinations would take the lives of presidential hopeful Robert Kennedy and civil rights leader Martin Luther King, Jr. Even the one government agency that made everything they did look so easy … NASA … faced grim reality when the three-man crew scheduled to fly the first Apollo mission died in a fire on the launch pad during a ground test. To be sure, there were still sitcoms and dramas coming into America's households, but they were starting to deal with more contemporary issues. It would reach its climax with "The Great Purge of 1971," when the new head of CBS cancelled programming he regarded as "hick" and "rural." Nineteen-seventy-one is recognized as the transitional year when the previously taboo topics of divorce, homosexuality, premarital sex, conservative/liberal political discussions and other issues came out of the closet and into TV programming.

Things were *much* different from the days of JFK's "Camelot." In 1961, Dick Van Dyke came through the door, tripped over a stool and fell into the arms of his adoring wife and smiling friends. President John Kennedy told us the "torch had been passed to a new generation" and if we put our minds to it, we could do anything. When *Good Morning World* went off the air in 1968, it seemed as if the country was hellbent on tearing itself apart.

After its cancellation, *Good Morning World* continued throughout the summer of 1968 in reruns, getting pre-empted here and there for the usual sprinkling of specials and for the networks' live coverage of both the Republican and Democratic political conventions. On September 17, the last episode aired and the new TV season began.

In the end, Ronnie Schell was disappointed.

Julie Parrish cried.

Billy De Wolfe shrugged his shoulders and told everyone to move forward. "Put it away, people, put it away," he would often advise the younger actors, meaning for them to stash some of their salaries away for that inevitable time when every series would end.

Goldie Hawn had moved onto *Rowan & Martin's Laugh-In*.
Joby Baker was bitter but relieved it was all behind him.
The Doris Day Show replaced *Good Morning World* in the Tuesday 9:30 p.m. time slot the following week. It would enjoy a successful five-year run that would take it through the summer of 1973.

Photo courtesy CBS/Paramount

It didn't take long for the former stars of *Good Morning World* to move forward with their careers. Less than a year after its cancellation, Joby Baker turned up in an early *Laugh-In* with Goldie Hawn. From there, it was on to movie roles like 1968's *Blackbeard's Ghost* and *Superdad* with Bob Crane in 1973. Television was still his strong suit and throughout the seventies and early eighties he could also be seen in TV movies like *Cry Rape* in 1973 and *The City* in 1977.

Guest appearances on other TV shows kept him visible to audiences in the years after *Good Morning World*; though he appeared in a few sitcoms, it was the crime and medical dramas that captured his attention. *Mannix, Barnaby Jones, Medical Center, Simon & Simon* and *Police Story* were some of the shows that showcased his talents. However, it was when he appeared on Jack Klugman's crime drama series that he felt he was at his best. "I loved working for Klugman," Baker remembered of his guest appearances on *Quincy* between 1977 and 1982. "When I worked with him, I was kinda great … I mean, he brought out the best in me. I don't know what he did, but that was some good times for me."

Baker's last regular role was in the short-lived 1980 series *The Six O'Clock Follies*, where he played Col. Harry Marvin. By the middle of the decade, Baker had all but dropped out of sight.

His partner on *Good Morning World* went back to being a Marine on *Gomer Pyle, U.S.M.C.*, and even got a step up in rank to Corporal. Ronnie Schell also had a recur-

Photo courtesy CBS/Paramount

ring role in the other Persky/Denoff TV show that was on the air, playing Ann Marie's agent on *That Girl*. Both shows ended in 1969 and 1971 respectively and Schell moved into supporting roles in several Disney feature films and TV specials in the coming decade, like 1975's *The Strongest Man in the World*, *The Shaggy D.A.* and *Gus* in 1976, *The Cat from Outer Space* from 1978 and 1981's *The Devil and Max Devlin*. Schell also worked in *The Mouseketeers at Walt Disney World* in 1977. But it was in doing voice characterization for children's shows and cartoons that Schell struck gold.

In 1973, Schell appeared as "Gilly" in *Goober and the Ghost Chasers*. That same year, he was a voice on *Butch Cassidy and the Sundance Kids*. Later in the decade, Schell's talents were in even more demand as he did voice work for other syndicated cartoons ... *Fred Flintstone and Friends* (1977), *Casper and the Angels* (1979) and *The Smurfs* (1981). The next step in his career came when, instead of doing anonymous multiple voices, he began doing specific characters like "Rick Raccoon" in 1982's *Shirt Tales*, "Freako the Ghost" in *Scooby Do Meets the Boo Brothers* in 1987, "Colonel Calloway" a year later in *Scooby-Doo and the Ghoul School* and "Rudy 2" in the 1990 movie version of the classic cartoon series *The Jetsons*. The one that brought him the most notoriety, however, was a 1987 animated series. "Casey Kasem and I made a show called *Battle of the Planets*," he said of the popular syndicated series. "He and I played a couple of young kids and my character was a seventeen-year-old!" Schell always had a youthful sound to his voice and two decades later, he still gets calls to voice younger-sounding characters in cartoons and commercials.

Throughout the nineties he appeared in other supporting roles in both TV and movies and, in 2002, was cast in a role he hadn't done since *Good Morning World*. In *The Biggest Fan*, he appeared as disc jockey Wiezel Wastedberg ... a far cry from his days playing playboy bachelor DJ Larry Clark back in 1967.

After *Good Morning World's* cancellation, Billy De Wolfe appeared with ex-*F-Troop* co-star Larry Storch in the brief TV series *The Queen and I*. He also kept the late night viewers awake with frequent guest appearances on *The Tonight Show* between 1970 and 1972. The following year he went right back to work in the familiar Tuesday evening 9:30 time slot ...

Photo courtesy CBS/Paramount

as Doris Martin's boss Willard Jarvis on *The Doris Day Show*, the very show that replaced his *Good Morning World*. De Wolfe and Day were lifelong friends and he was the perfect addition to her series. Throughout the remainder of his career, he appeared with Bob Crane in the 1969 television remake of the classic *Arsenic and Old Lace* in the role of Officer O'Hara and is probably best remembered today as the voice of the evil Professor Hinkle in the perennial animated holiday favorite *Frosty the Snowman*.

De Wolfe was by now in his late sixties and a lifelong cigarette smoker. In late 1973, he was cast as "Madame Lucy," a foppish dress designer in the Broadway musical *Irene*, which starred Debbie Reynolds. It was a role reminiscent of his "Mrs. Murgatroyd" days from years earlier. However, he had been diagnosed with lung cancer and when his health began to deteriorate, he had to withdraw from the pre-Broadway auditions. George Irving replaced him in the show and went on to win the Tony Award for Best Supporting Actor in a Musical for 1974. There is no doubt that De Wolfe would have won it as well.

Less than two weeks after his sixty-seventh birthday, Billy De Wolfe ... William Jones ... passed away from lung cancer on March 5, 1974.

Photo courtesy CBS/Paramount

He is buried in his family's plot in Quincy, Massachusetts at Mt. Wollaston Cemetery. His gravestone says "William A. Jones A.K.A. Billy De Wolfe ... February 18, 1907 - March 5, 1974."

After *Good Morning World*'s demise, the now twenty-seven-year-old Julie Parrish made the rounds in guest appearances on various TV shows and made numerous commercials in the later part of the decade, representing on screen clients like Ajax Detergent, Sterling Beer and National Airlines. Not allowing herself to be limited to television or movies, Parrish also continued working in live theatre throughout the seventies and eighties; in fact, it was due to the rave reviews she received in Arthur Miller's *After the Fall* that she landed the role in *Good Morning World*. She was also involved with a comedy improv group on and off for six years during that time. In addition to a pair of appearances each on *Mannix*, *The Rockford Files* and *Dynasty*, she also was a regular for the first season of 1972's *Return to Peyton Place*, playing the role of Betty Anderson Harrington Cord and had a three-year run as Maggie Brady in the early eighties series *Capitol*. There were movie roles as well; *The Doberman Gang* from 1972, *The Devil and Max Devlin*, where she teamed up with her former co-star Ronnie Schell in 1981; and made-for-TV movies such as 1978's *The Time Machine* and *The Last Fling* from 1987.

She added writing to her resume too, not only appearing in an episode of *Laverne & Shirley*, but writing one as well. And although it didn't spawn any hits, she recorded an album of country music in the late eighties. "When We Dance" didn't receive much airplay from radio stations, but was a great showcase of Parrish's vocal talents.

Which brings us to the person who benefitted the most from the exposure her first TV series brought her. Without *Good Morning World* Goldie Hawn would've never gotten that breakout role in *Rowan & Martin's Laugh-In*. And without *Laugh-In*, it's difficult to say how long it would have taken Goldie Hawn to catapult to stardom the way she did.

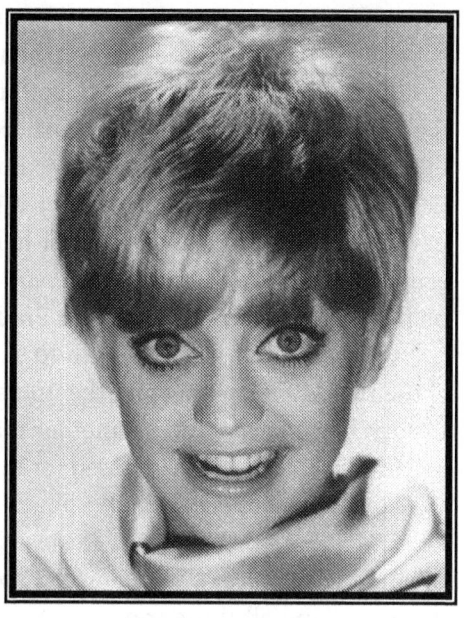

Photo courtesy CBS/Paramount

Joby Baker was correct in his opinion that Hawn was on a "Goldie Hawn star mission" since while establishing a presence in *Laugh-In*, she immediately launched into her first feature film, playing a dancer in 1968's *The One and Only, Genuine, Original Family Band*. A year later, that *Laugh-In* charisma paid off when she was cast opposite Walter Matthau in *Cactus Flower*, where she won the Oscar for Best Supporting Actress in April 1970. Ronnie Schell recalled his "Watch and learn from the master" pep talk with the actress from just a couple of years earlier.

"She watched and learned all right," he joked in hindsight. "I watched and learned she'd won the Academy Award while I was working some little dinner theatre in Omaha, Nebraska." Did she indeed "learn from the master?"

"She sure did ... and I never let her forget it."

After winning the Oscar for her performance in *Cactus Flower*, Hawn's resume is a long list of motion pictures familiar to any moviegoer; the ditzy blonde role would be reprised in 1970's *There's a Girl in My Soup* and *Butter-*

flies Are Free from 1972. By the middle of the decade, though, Hawn was showing those inside and outside the Hollywood beltway that her acting abilities went far deeper.

She was a desperate mother on the run in 1974's *The Sugarland Express;* in 1975, she handily showed just how multi-talented she was in *Shampoo* with Warren Beatty, *Foul Play* in 1978 and then earning another Oscar nomination (Best Actress) for her starring role in *Private Benjamin* in 1980, which spawned a later TV series. Throughout the eighties, films like *Best Friends* (1982), *Protocol* and *Swing Shift*, both from 1984, and 1987's *Overboard* further enhanced her visibility as a major film star and marketability as someone who touches a movie and turns it into box office gold. During the nineties, she was also able to prove her capacity as both producer and director, developing and producing some of her own film projects, beginning as executive producer on *Private Benjamin*. Her name can be seen in the credits on many of her films as "Executive Producer."

As she moved from strength to strength, by 1995 *Empire Magazine* had chosen Goldie Hawn as one the 100 sexiest movie stars in motion picture history. Eleven years earlier another magazine recognized her talents. At the age of thirty-nine, she had posed for the cover of *Playboy*. Even though there were guest appearances on talk shows like *The Tonight Show, Late Night with David Letterman, Oprah, The Rosie O'Donnell Show* ... even a guest shot on the irreverent *Space Ghost Coast to Coast,* numerous TV specials through the decade ... and all those movies dating back to 1969, she's probably remembered best for those years she spent giggling and mugging through all the gags on *Rowan and Martin's Laugh-In*.

The "star mission" paid off even though after *Good Morning World* life has not been without its challenges. There was a pair of failed marriages, one to Gus Trikonis from 1969 to 1976 and the other to the Hudson Brothers' comedy team brother Bill Hudson from 1976 to 1979. That marriage produced two children, Oliver and Kate Hudson. Daughter Kate would go on to be a successful actress in her own right and both would later become involved with their mother in the formation of a production company called Cosmic Entertainment in 2003. By 1983, Goldie became the longtime companion, but not the wife, of former Disney child star Kurt Russell. To their credit, the couple has been together longer than most Hollywood marriages and welcomed son Wyatt Russell into the family in 1986. In the early nineties, she juggled her career with being a caregiver to her ailing mother, who died in 1994. Family life returned full-circle in early 2004 when Kate Hudson and her husband Chris Robinson announced they were having a baby, which would make Goldie Hawn a grandmother at the age of sixty. All things considered, life has been very good for Goldie Hawn.

Finally, what about the patron saints of *Good Morning World* ... Bill Persky and Sam Denoff? Denoff admits that the duo really wasn't prepared to produce and manage two TV shows at the same time so it was a good thing that *Good Morning World* ended when it did. Their other concoction, Marlo Thomas' *That Girl*, continued on the air on ABC until 1971, but no one ... not even Persky and Denoff ... could imagine what an impact *That Girl* would have on a generation of teen girls and young women. It and *The Mary Tyler Moore Show* became cultural icons.

The tables would be turned somewhat seven years later when Persky & Denoff found themselves working for their former supporting actress. Goldie Hawn asked the pair to write for an upcoming TV production of hers. The 1978 *Goldie Hawn Special* went a long way in showing to viewers ... and to Persky & Denoff ... that the nervous dancer that brought the teacup to her audition had indeed grown up.

After wrapping up *Good Morning World,* Sam Denoff continued to write and produce several shows with Bill Persky in the seventies and eighties, employing their talents in the TV series *The Funny Side, Lotsa Luck, Big Eddie* and *The Montefuscos*. He was also a writer/producer for the 1991 series *Harry and the Hendersons,* as well as a writer for the 1995 special *50 Years of Funny Females* and 2000's *The 14th Annual American Comedy Awards.*

You can also catch him in front of the camera, too. He's the gas station attendant in 1974's *Roll, Freddy Roll*, the art dealer in the 1990 made-for-TV reunion movie *Return to Green Acres,* "Father Farrell" in an episode of 2003's *Life with Bonnie* and as "Lord Jerome" in *The Princess Diaries* (2001) and the 2004 sequel *The Princess Diaries 2: Royal Engagement.*

Today, he is semi-retired and lives in Los Angeles, neighbors with his old buddy Ronnie Schell.

His former partner, Bill Persky, lives in Manhattan and still is active in both producing and directing. In addition to writing and producing duties with Denoff on shows already mentioned, Persky continued on as a director, a position he had held since the early days of *That Girl*. His name appears in the credits as director in TV shows like 1973's *Here We Go Again, Welcome Back, Kotter* from 1975, *The Practice* and *Alice*, both from 1976, and a trio of shows that defined TV in the mid-eighties; *Kate & Allie, Spencer: For Hire* and *Who's the Boss.*

Today, he readily admits that "I dabble in a lot of stuff, but I basically don't do nuthin'... and there isn't enough time to get it all done." That "dabbling" involved writing a pilot for a TV series for NBC in the 2004 season that didn't sell and helping to bring along another generation of writers ... nurturing them like Carl Reiner and Sheldon Leonard did with he and Denoff years before. "I write and I teach a lot of young kids that I mentor and help ... and I basically just hang out."

Looking back, maybe *Good Morning World's* cancellation wasn't such a bad deal after all. All one has to do is type any of their names into an Internet search engine (imdb.com is a great source!) and it's evident that their lives and careers did go on after *Good Morning World* got the axe.

But as we'll see in the next and final chapters, sometimes those lives and careers didn't quite go in the direction expected ...

Chapter 6:

A Look Back ...

Ten years after *Good Morning World* went off the air another TV series about a radio station made its debut on CBS. In the fall of 1978, *WKRP in Cincinnati* entered the territory pioneered by *Good Morning World* ... with almost the same results. Suffering from anemic ratings, CBS pulled *WKRP* off the air after only eight episodes. On hiatus for two months, the series reappeared in January 1979 with a flashback episode to reacquaint old viewers and introduce the show to new ones. The scheme worked and *WKRP in Cincinnati* enjoyed a successful four-year run. Audiences ate up being able to see what must be going on behind the scenes of their favorite radio stations ... and those of us that were on the air appreciated the show's realistic approach to the industry we were working in.

Just as Bill Persky and Sam Denoff based their *Good Morning World* premise on the antics of the old Klavan and Finch show on WNEW, *WKRP in Cincinnati* creator Hugh Wilson based his show on a real-life station too. And contrary to popular belief, it wasn't my former employer WKRC in Cincinnati. Wilson told me when I interviewed him back in 1990 that the idea came to him after talking to some friends that worked at WQXI in Atlanta ..."Quixie in Dixie" ... back in the late sixties.

Wilson said that at that time there was a morning guy who had a resume as long as your arm due to all the stations he had been fired from (Dr. Johnny Fever); a buxom blonde secretary, who was *really* the one who kept things going at the station (Jennifer Marlow); a program director that wandered in one day from a state out west (Andy Travis); a befuddled newsman, who always had a bandage stuck somewhere on his face (Les Nessman); a salesman ... pardon me, account executive ... who always had a deal in the works (Herb Tarlick); and a station manager who would do anything for you but didn't have a clue what was going on (Arthur Carlson, the Big Guy). All of *WKRP's* characters had their basis in some real person at Quixie in Dixie. They were all mirror images of people like us who were lucky enough to be radio DJ's. If there weren't enough viewers out there watching to keep *WKRP* on the air, those of us that were actually working at radio stations would be more than happy to make up the difference. *WKRP's* Thanksgiving episode is legendary!

Photo courtesy CBS/MTM Productions

It was in 1978 that Desilu closed its doors to their Cahuenga Boulevard studios. In hindsight, it's hard to believe that this little studio had only five stages but practically all the shows that had been produced there were in the top ten at one time or another. When Bill Persky heard the doors were closing, he went over to the old lots where he and Sam Denoff plied their trade so long before. And like many of us who have ever been to a sale for someone we knew, Persky was looking for a memento to take home. "The studio closed and they were having a sale of all the props and things of that sort," Persky remembered. He and Sam Denoff decided to go to the sale and take a look around. With a little luck, maybe they'd find a memento of some show they had worked on. Persky recalled there being literally hundreds of lamps, chairs and other types of furniture and props up for sale. But then he stumbled across something that caused a smile to blend in with a flood of memories.

"As I was walking around, I came across this lamp," Persky said, "and on it was a piece of tape with one of Joby's lines on it." The old prop from *Good Morning World* brought back memories of how much Baker hated the staging being changed. "He'd go nuts when we did that. He'd go around tacking dialogue up on the wall, on doors ... anywhere he could!" Persky couldn't help but laugh under his breath as he examined one of the few things that survived from his old show.

Has it really been that long ago? I'm afraid it has. All of us, from the producers, directors, writers and performers who put the show on the air all the way down to a ten-year-old boy, who got into radio because of it, have gotten older. Persky, Denoff, Schell and Baker are in their seventies. Goldie Hawn is in her sixties and at one time used her influence to prevent the series from being released into syndication in the mid-seventies, feeling it would be detrimental to her image at the time and not a true reflection of her abilities as an actress. (And *Laugh-In* is?) While the series may have appeared in syndication on individual stations over the years, it didn't enjoy true national distribution until USA Network aired it as part of a package of comedies during the summer of 1986. In January 2006, the series was released on DVD. All twenty-six episodes were re-mastered and cleaned up. Unfortunately, the original Rifkin/Farrell pilot couldn't be located. It's a good thing the show has found its final resting place on DVD since the original films were all degrading, looking tinged with a dull red as the film emulsion breaks down.

When the series was on the air, Julie Parrish was in what Bill Persky described as a "hot" relationship with her pre-*Godfather* boyfriend James Caan. The pair was inseparable, despite movie producer Hal Wallis, *Star Trek's* William Shatner and *Batman* himself, Adam West, trying to put the moves on her and break up the couple. When the break-up did occur, Parrish hooked up with actor Ted Bessel following *That Girl's* cancellation. It wouldn't be a pleasant experience for the then-thirty-three-year-old actress.

Her relationship with Bessel became violent and abusive, with tabloids and newspapers alike reporting on her being victimized by "verbal abuse" by Bessel. There were even gossip columns reporting on her checking into a hospital with bruises and cuts, although these were never confirmed. Parrish's experiences with Bessel left a lasting impression and in the late eighties and throughout the nineties, she was elected to the Board of Directors of the Los Angeles Commission on Assaults Against Women and worked on their Crisis Hotline as well. She invested nine years of her life as a full time on-staff counselor at the Haven Hills Shelter for Battered Women, a crisis intervention center for abused women and their children. In the late nineties Parrish began undergraduate studies, eventually earning a degree in chemical dependencies counseling.

Parrish's greatest battle would be a fight her body would wage against itself. In 1993, she was diagnosed with ovarian cancer and battled it twice successfully throughout the decade. She underwent surgery and chemotherapy in 1993 and, embracing a vegetarian diet, became the classic story of a survivor. The disease returned in 1999 and Parrish was forced to have surgery a second time and endure more chemotherapy. In the ensuing years whenever she was at a speaking engagement, Parrish would speak honestly and openly on not only her experiences as an abused woman but she also would encourage others in their fight against cancer.

As the new century began, Parrish traveled the country appearing at conventions and trade shows, signing autographs and talking with fans. Sometimes it would be a pleasant surprise when a young man would ask for an autograph and then strike up a conversation about her days on *Good Morning World*. Memories of her old show always brought a smile to her face.

Parrish was looking forward to her sixty-third birthday on October 21, 2003. She and *Good Morning World* co-star Ronnie Schell were appearing at a convention in Knoxville, Tennessee in early September, signing autographs and catching up on old times. Whether she was aware of it or not, the cancer was back and in the next few weeks her health would start to decline rapidly.

Photo courtesy Bruce Button

Ronnie Schell remembered how he felt the day he heard Julie Parrish had died.

"We had worked in an autograph show about a month before she died, around Labor Day weekend," Schell recalled. "She had had cancer for something like ten years and had recovered well, but I heard one night she went to bed and died in her sleep … that's the way I want to go."

Julie Parrish died on October 1, 2003, just twenty days shy of her sixty-third birthday, at Tarzana Community Hospital. Her brother reported she had passed away of natural causes that no doubt stemmed from her history of ovarian cancer.

Ronnie Schell and Sam Denoff both spoke at Parrish's memorial service a little over three weeks later, kindly remembering their fellow performer and comforting the grieving family. Death would touch Schell again in late March 2005 with the passing of his mother at the age of ninety-two.

Unlike a lot of actors who do all they can to beat the aging process, the now seventy-five-year-old Ronnie Schell seems to have embraced it. Part of that acceptance began years before when he was doing *Gomer Pyle, U.S.M.C.* "I think you have to take care of yourself physically and mentally," he shared, remembering a director he had worked with on the set. "I noticed a producer, who was Aaron Reuben, was in fairly good shape and he was in his sixties then." Reuben told the actor that his secret to staying vital was a daily swimming routine. "So while I was doing *Gomer Pyle* I started swimming every day and have been doing so ever since." Recently Schell has added weightlifting for seniors to his exercise regimen and pays close attention to his diet. All of it has paid off for an actor who admits to never aspiring to stardom but being content just to work in his chosen craft. And in his senior years, he is still busy.

"I have actually had gray hair for over twenty-five years and I used to put a little color on it," Schell admitted. "But in the last couple of years I've let it go completely white and I'm getting more offers for work now than I got in the last ten or twelve years."

At the time of this writing, Ronnie Schell is going strong and headlining an extended-run live dinner theatre production in Palm Springs, California. Entitled "Senior Class," it celebrates the fact that there is life beyond retirement.

"Up until now, I've never done a booked musical and this production at Palm Desert is all about the positive side of senior life." The musical comedy is written from the sense that when older people enjoy the performance they leave with the feeling of 'Hey, it's not all bad being a senior citizen!' Appearing

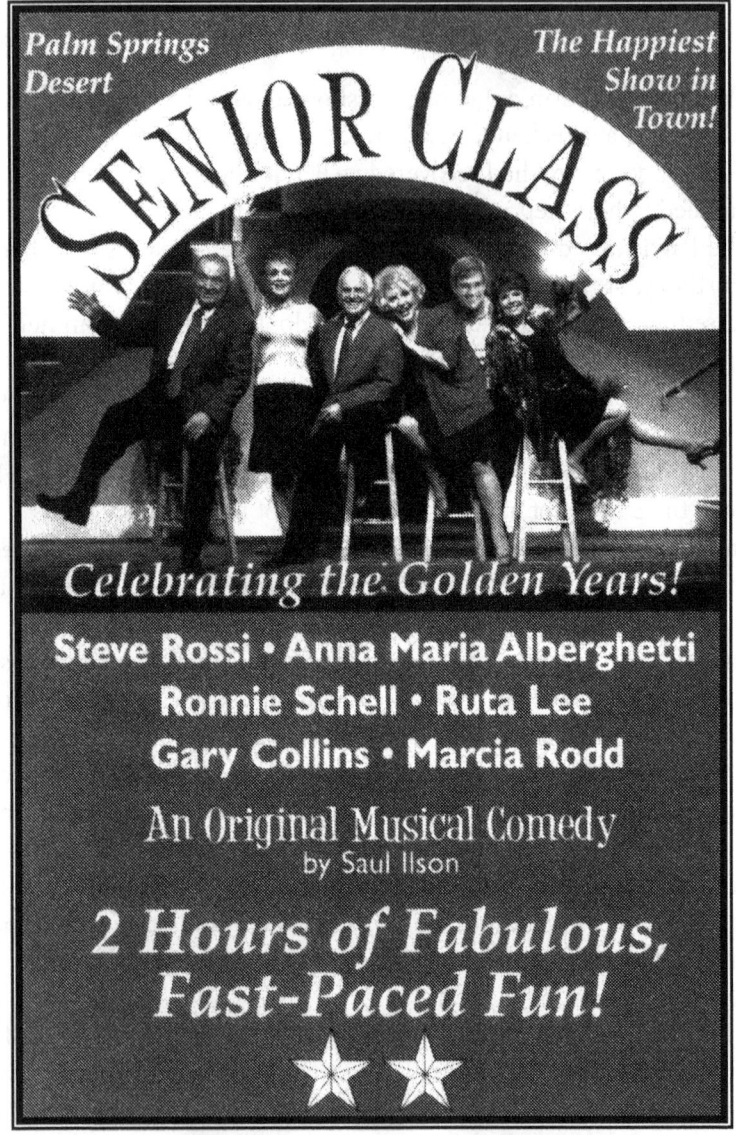

Senior Class Flyer courtesy Ronnie Schell/Palm Desert

with Schell is a host of familiar names from the past; Anna Maria Alberghetti, Julius LaRosa, Steve Rossi and Ruta Lee.

As for retirement any time soon? For Ronnie Schell, it isn't in his future plans. "I don't think I'm gonna retire … all my friends are retired and other than playing golf and tending flowers I ask them 'what do you do all day?'… and they have problems giving me an answer." Schell related that part of being in show business is that as one ages, he or she moves into a different status, allowing the actor to play the role of a senior citizen. "You can keep working for as long as you want, so as long as I'm physically and mentally able to, I'll keep at it."

The show book that is given to patrons when they come to see *Senior Class* has a quote penned by Schell that sums up his feelings on his career up till now; "This is a dividend that came late in my life and I hope I live long enough to enjoy it!"

For Joby Baker ... star of stage, screen and television ... the magic just ran out. The actor was seriously burned out with show business. It was as if he were living a moment from the 2000 Mel Gibson made-for-TV movie, *The Three Stooges*. In one scene, Larry Fine is walking on the beach with Moe Howard, lamenting about how their careers had turned out. "I think we've stayed at the dance too long," he tells Moe. "It just isn't fun anymore." That was how it felt in Baker's case.

"I never looked forward to getting up in the morning and going to work," Baker remembered both of his days on *Good Morning World* and the years that followed. For *Good Morning World* in particular, Baker places much of the blame for its shortcomings on himself. "I don't like to say they made it tough for me, I probably made it tough for myself." Baker thinks that if the situation of the show had been written better and more forethought applied, it would've been a better series that might have enjoyed a longer run than just one season. "I don't wanna lay it all on Bill and Sam since I think a lot of it was my own fault."

Baker began dreading going on auditions. "I used to take rejection personally, I mean, I really had a problem," he recalled of the years that followed *Good Morning World*. "I know actors who would go and not get parts fifty out of a hundred times or more and they couldn't care less." Baker took the rejections to heart and the more rejection he experienced, the harder it became reading for other roles. "For a long time it really bothered me and in looking back, I don't know what I was doing in that business and it surprises me I got as far as I did." Through sheer talent and ability, Baker was able to pull it off and even fooled himself. Bill Persky echoed his sentiments and admitted that in hindsight he missed an important signal regarding Baker's performance.

"Joby was on a *Van Dyke* show before we hired him for *Good Morning World*," he said in retrospect. "And he was great on it, don't get me wrong, but I edited that episode and really lost track of how much editing I had to do to make him look that good." Persky remembers pulling up a few frames here, cutting out a few there and being off of Baker for a line that he didn't do well.

"I think the editing fooled all of us and he came across with all the charm he was capable of."

The final product that went on the air conveyed an easygoing, in charge and utterly charming actor. What Persky, Denoff and Reiner forgot about was the ten to fifteen hours in the editing room it took to make him look that way.

The last straw in Baker's discontent with not only the entertainment industry but life itself came about in 1985. Earlier in the decade, his marriage to actress Joan Blackman had ended in divorce. By the mid-eighties, he was remarried to Dory Previn, ex-wife of noted composer/musician Andre Previn. Baker never enjoyed going on interviews and auditions and now a middle-aged actor in his early fifties, he had grown to detest them. One day, something snapped.

"We were in our home in Nichols Canyon up in Hollywood Hills and I was getting ready to go to Warner Brothers to read for a part," Baker said of the watershed event. He moped and complained as he got ready that morning, mentioning to his wife what was on tap for the day. It was plain to Dory that something was bothering her husband and she asked him if he was happy doing what he did for a living. Baker admitted, in his words, that he "hated doing this anymore." She then posed a question to him that literally changed his life from that day forward.

"How do you see yourself?" she asked thoughtfully. "As a painter who acts, or an actor who paints?" Baker's response was the former and to that his wife gave him some advice... so simple that a child could understand it. "She told me, 'Then don't do it anymore'... and I quit right then and there and never acted again, and kept working as an artist." True to his word, Baker's filmography and acting career ended in the mid-eighties.

Today, Joby Baker enjoys the notoriety of an accomplished artist who sells and exhibits his works throughout New England and in museums in New York. When viewing reruns of *Good Morning World*, check out the paintings that are hanging on the walls of Dave and Linda's apartment. All are from the brush of Joby Baker.

To give you an idea of how far Baker dropped off the radar of show business, when doing the research for this book it was clear to me that it wouldn't be complete unless he was a part of it. But no one knew where he had moved to. My conversations with the cast and crew of the show proved fruitless, even the Screen Actors Guild had no clue where he lived.

One day while searching Ebay for something unrelated, I happened across a print that was up for auction from a New York City art gallery painted by none other than Baker. Figuring I had nothing to lose except a 39 cent stamp, I wrote a letter to the gallery explaining who I was and what I was writing and asked them if they'd be so kind as to forward the letter to Baker. I was very clear that I didn't want to intrude where I wasn't welcome and if he didn't want to be a part of my book, I'd understand. (I kept my fingers crossed since I knew this book was dead in the water without *Good Morning World*'s other lead star!)

That was right before Memorial Day weekend and when I returned to work the following Tuesday at the college I was teaching at, there was a memo in my mail box…from none other than some guy named Joby Baker! To make a long story short, I found Joby to be a kindred spirit who was frank and honest in his comments, and a terrific fellow artist who gave me a standing invitation to visit him and his wife in their New England studio. Maybe I can give him some tips concerning his artwork…

The couple abandoned the show business culture of Southern California and traded it for a one-hundred-acre estate in Massachusetts. If you plot it out on a map of the United States, you couldn't get any further away if you tried. Baker has a small studio for his artistic endeavors and Dory a studio of her own in the opposite end of the house for her writing and musical pursuits. They stay pretty much to themselves, with Baker admitting that he and his wife have a few close friends that they are immensely loyal to and care for deeply. Today, the pace of life is more relaxed than those days when he was a "big star." Getting up in the morning isn't as difficult, either.

The now seventy-four-year-old former actor is content with his life on his New England ranch. In fact, some mornings he'll get up a little earlier than usual just so he can catch a glimpse of the sun's first rays over the landscape visible from his back porch deck. The artist in him appreciates the cascade of colors flooding his senses as he eases back in his chair and gently blows across the hot cup of coffee he's holding before taking his first sip. Without even thinking … and to no one in particular … Joby Baker greets the day in a whisper as only he can.

"Good morning world …"

www.ingramcontent.com/pod-product-compliance
Lightning Source LLC
Chambersburg PA
CBHW072200160426
43197CB00012B/2468